Whitey on the Moon:
Race, Politics, and the Death of the US Space Program,
1958–1972

PAUL KERSEY

WHITEY ON THE MOON

RACE, POLITICS, AND THE DEATH OF THE US SPACE PROGRAM, 1958–1972

ANTELOPE HILL PUBLISHING

Dedicated to Chuck Yeager

Contents

1

"I Saw No Minorities or Women as Astronauts. Could I Help Make a Difference?"

July 8th, 2014

"I'm never just talking about people being nice to each other. I'm talking about changing the system," she told a civil rights oral history interviewer for Howard University in 1971. "We ought to have one big coalition . . . [of African Americans and] . . . all our minorities [with which] we could change anything in this system."

— Ruth Bates Harris[1]

I saw no minorities or women as astronauts. Could I help make a difference?

— Ruth Bates Harris, *Harlem Princess*, 248

Thoughts sometimes stray away from the madness of reality, allowing a momentary, fantastical glimpse into the old "what might have been" mindset.

With today's date being July 8th, 2014, at the time of writing, I think back to what Americans were thinking on this date in 1969.

Forty-five years ago.

Eight days from the launch of Apollo 11.

---

[1] Ruth Bates Harris, deputy assistant administrator for equal opportunity (NASA's highest ranking Black female), in Dick and Launius, *Societal Impact of Spaceflight*, 427.

Twelve days from the landing on the Moon.

What were their hopes and dreams for the future, especially considering my parents were roughly between the ages of eight and fourteen?

Did they envision men and women living in colonies on the Moon, a spaceport for further exploration of the heavens?

Did they ever believe that eighty-four people (fourteen killed) would be shot over a July 4th weekend in one American city (well, calling Chicago an American city is a stretch at this point)?[2]

Did they, in their wildest dreams, believe the United States government would actively promote the dissolution of the majority (founding) population via aggressively deciding to forgo its duty to protect our borders?

Did they understand the safeguards their grandparents' generation had put into law (restrictive covenants, segregation of public schools, and freedom of association protecting small businesses' right to discriminate) were there to ensure stability and promote tranquility?

It was never about racism.

Now we know it was about protecting civilization.

But to be able to look upon the Moon on July 8th, 1969, knowing no man had ever set foot upon it (and the wonderment of what would come after they did) is a thought I'd trade anything for at this point.

For we live in a world where we now know what came next: the abandonment of space exploration for the ceaseless, never-ending promotion of Blacks (and now all racial minorities and aggrieved special interest groups).

And in the forty-five years since we first went to the Moon, the trillions of dollars (and untold hundreds of trillions of opportunity costs) spent on this constant and ongoing campaign to dismantle our civilization to the benefit of Blacks has—if you open your eyes up for only a moment—produced example

---

[2] In Chicago, 2014.

after example after example showing that our ancestors knew far more than we did about race.

Though will never know what truly went through his mind, Deke Slayton was perhaps the most important man behind the success of NASA from 1962 to 1972 (the era before diversity became the primary goal of the space agency instead of, you know, space exploration). Slayton was the voice of the Mercury astronauts, the man who selected the crews who flew the Gemini, Apollo, and Skylab missions.

Deke! U.S. Manned Space: From Mercury to the Shuttle is the story of Donald K. "Deke" Slayton, an autobiography of a man whose greatness is an embarrassment to our generation.

In his book, Deke explains how the astronautical candidates were selected in an era before Black women (with a huge racial chip on their shoulder) like Ruth Bates Harris came to lord over NASA and derail our space efforts—momentarily—for the promotion of the same people who would inherit Detroit via White flight and turn it into—Detroit.

This is how Deke describes how astronauts were selected, and how even in 1962 the federal government was working to promote Blacks as the primary goal of every mission:

> All the while the astronaut selection process continued. We had known going into the 1962 selection that we would need more astronauts at some point in the future, so as the nine new guys completed their initial training, we decided to pick up some more.
>
> Gemini was always intended to consist of ten or eleven manned flights—that was a minimum of twenty seats right there. Then you had Apollo, which in at that point called for the following:
>
> Four manned Apollo earth orbit missions launched with the Saturn I rocket beginning in 1965.
>
> Two to four manned Apollo earth orbit missions on the Saturn IB beginning in 1966.
>
> At least six manned earth and lunar orbit missions on the Saturn V beginning in 1967.

All this was designed to lead up to a manned lunar landing in 1968–1969.

The procedure and qualifications were pretty similar to
the recruitment for the 1962 group, though we dropped the
test pilot requirement, figuring we had just about drained
the pool. Applicants with operational flying backgrounds or
advanced degrees in related areas would be accepted. It was
with this selection, however, that I got caught in my first,
last, and only political battle over astronaut selection.

The Kennedy Administration, particularly the President's brother, Robert, thought there should be a black astronaut. The Navy didn't have anyone remotely qualified,
but in the Air Force there was a black bomber pilot, Captain
Edward Dwight, who had applied for Yeager's Aerospace
Research Pilot School (ARPS).

The trouble was, his multiengine background, lack of an
engineering degree, and lack of the normal test pilot school
caused him to be ranked pretty far down the list of applicants. (The school normally enrolled eight at a time.)

The pressure started with General LeMay, who was ordered by Bobby Kennedy to get Dwight enrolled at ARPS.
Yeager resisted—it wasn't about racism, it was just that according to the rankings, Dwight had finished in the middle
of the pack. Yeager thought it would be reverse racism to
enroll Dwight ahead of pilots with better qualifications.

They worked out a deal: Dwight would be enrolled, but
so would all those pilots on the list ahead of him. That's why
that year the ARPS had a class of fourteen rather than
eight.

Dwight got through the school and did okay, even though
Yeager brought in a tutor for him, all of that. But okay
wasn't really enough. Remember, NASA wasn't just looking
at the ARPS graduates as potential astronauts: our pool included the Navy and the Marines, civilian pilots and now
research scientists, not to mention other Air Force pilots and
test pilots, some of whom had really proved themselves in
flight test. These were guys like Michael Collins, a good applicant for the 1962 group who had been held back to get

another year experience. Or Dick Gordon, who was one of the Navy's best pilots.

As I hear it, Dwight himself wasn't particularly driven to become an astronaut.

I had already developed a point system that we used in making the final evaluations on astronaut candidates. There were three parts: academic, pilot performance, and character/motivation, ten points for each part, with thirty being the highest possible score. Some of it was cut-and-dry: you got points for a certain amount of flying and for education. Some of it, by design, was subjective and based on face-to-face interviews. Just based on the flying and technical matters, Dwight finished out of the running.[3]

Merit: this was what built America.

The promotion of those without merit, but with melanin: this is what has helped bring America to her knees.

It's important to note Andrew Chaikin's book *A Man on the Moon: The Voyages of the Apollo Astronauts* includes a powerful note about the character of Deke.

In the author's notes, Chaikin writes:

However, civil rights had briefly become an issue within the astronaut corps in 1963. A black pilot named Ed Dwight, who had barely graduated from Chuck Yeager's space school, had applied for the astronaut program and been rejected. The astronauts were on a desert-survival course in Nevada when Slayton was summoned for a phone call from Washington. When he returned, he told the other astronauts that he had just spoken to Attorney General Robert Kennedy, who wanted NASA to accept Dwight. Slayton told the pilots, "I just spoke for all you guys. . . . I said if we had to take him and he wasn't qualified, then they'd have to find sixteen other people, because all of us would leave."[4]

---

[3] Slayton and Cassutt, *Deke!*, 132–3.
[4] Andrew Chaikin, *A Man on the Moon*, 625.

Character, in the face of a Kennedy Administration dedicated to the proposition that only Black people were equal in the pursuit of justice.

One of the three men on board Apollo 11, Michael Collins, wrote in his *Carrying the Fire: An Astronaut's Journey* the following about Deke's system for evaluating potential candidates:

> Deke proposed a system which had been used in previous selections, and with minor modifications we agreed. It was a thirty-point system divided equally into three parts: academics, pilot performance, character and motivation. "Academics" was really a misnomer, as an examination of its components will reveal: IQ score—one point; academic degrees, honors, and other credentials—four points; results of NASA-administered aptitude tests—three points; and results of a technical interview—two points. Pilot performance broke down into: examination of flying records (total time, type of airplane, etc.)—three points; flying rating by test pilot school or other supervisors—one point; and results of technical interview—six points. Character and motivation was not subdivided, but the entire ten-point package was examined in the interview, and the victim's personality was an important part of it. Hence, of the thirty points, eighteen could be awarded during the all-important interview.[5]

Merit. This was how we went to the Moon.

It was no hoax, no more than building a railroad from one coast to the other or laying a wire to transmit cables from the North American continent to Europe was a hoax.

A much different civilization went to the Moon, just as a much different civilization helped turn the "Arsenal of Democracy" into a living, breathing experiment in racial realities in 2014.

---

[5] Collins, *Carrying the Fire*, 178–9.

Ruth Bates Harris' autobiography *Harlem Princess* triumphantly concludes with a depiction of congressional hearings
into the overwhelming Whiteness of NASA from 1962–1972.
It is this world we still live in:

> During the summer of 1972, concern about the lack of
> women and minorities in the astronaut program was partic-
> ularly strong. At the National Urban League convention
> during the first week of August, the absence of black, Chi-
> cano, and women astronauts was a topic of conversation. It
> was during this period that Representative Charles B.
> Rangel (D., New York) called upon the US Civil Rights Com-
> mission to conduct an investigation of NASA to determine
> why it had no , Spanish, or women astronauts. Rangel
> said: Something is seriously wrong when not a single mem-
> ber of the 42 man astronaut corps is female, Black or His-
> panic. During its 14-year history, NASA has had only one
> Black nominee to be an astronaut [he was Major Robert H.
> Lawrence with the AF MOL Program, who was killed in an
> F-104 aircraft accident before he had the opportunity to join
> NASA]. John Buggs, the newly appointed Staff Director of
> the US Civil Rights Commission, responded to Rangel by
> declaring that "an investigation of NASA would fall in line
> with the responsibility of the commission." As a result, Jef-
> frey M. Miller, Director, Office of Federal Civil Rights Eval-
> uation, told NASA in a letter written August 12th, 1972:
> "The commission recently received a letter from Congress-
> man Rangel which asserted that all of the astronauts in
> NASA's space program are white males. In view of the im-
> portant part that this program plays on our lives and the
> great psychological impact that media coverage of our
> manned space efforts has on millions or [sic] people around
> the world, this figure if true is most distressing.'"
> Miller asked for specific and detailed information on as-
> tronauts, to include race, ethnicity, and sex for past and pre-
> sent astronauts, a description of the manner in which they
> were selected and an explanation of minority and female un-
> derutilization, if such was the case: and NASA's detailed

plans for increasing the participation of minorities and women in the group selected for space missions.

On Friday, January 11th, 1975, Senator William Proxmire (D., Wisconsin), chairman of the Space Science and Veterans Committee, opened hearings to investigate operations of the NASA Equal Opportunity Office. Senator Proxmire stated that "nothing has exemplified NASA's achievement more than our astronaut program, and he properly recognized the fine character and achievement of the young astronauts. It has been not only the Agency's showpiece but indeed the country's showpiece." His concern, however, was that "the astronaut corps had no blacks or females currently in training as astronauts," Willis Shapley, NASA Associate Deputy Administrator, responded to Senator Proxmire in his testimony: "Mr. Chairman . . . I think the space program of that period may be criticized for not having taken aggressive enough measures to insure *[sic]* that there were qualified women and blacks and other minorities. . . . I should mention that the requirements and the preparation specifically . . . for the Shuttle program definitely include the provision for female astronauts."[6]

When you look back on the past forty-five years, the criticism of the White men who successfully administered and participated in the Apollo project—starting in 1973 by Ruth Bates Harris, whose stated goal was that "we ought to have one big coalition . . . [of African Americans and] . . . all our minorities [with which] we could change anything in this system"—should have served as a warning to any right-thinking person something was seriously rotten in the states of America.

Thoughts sometimes stray away from the madness of reality, allowing a momentary, fantastical glimpse into the old "what might have been" mindset.

With the date July 8th, 2014, I think back to what Americans were thinking on this date in July 8th, 1969.

---

6 Harris, *Harlem Princess*, 264–5.

Forty-five years ago.

Eight days from the launch of Apollo 11.

Twelve days from the landing on the Moon.

Today, our government actively floods this "nation" with a people who can only look upon the Moon and use its light as a guide to invade and flood our borders.

Our destiny is not Detroit.

It's not Baltimore.

It's not Newark, or the incredible savagery found in the Black parts of Chicago, where eighty-four people were shot over one July 4th weekend.

We must survive what's coming, to remind those who come after us of what they inherit and what they must safeguard for the future.

For the current state of the country is not it.

The current state of the United States of America is the fruition of Ruth Bates Harris' dream of a coalition of minorities rising together to dismantle what Whites built, and remake as their own (though they'll never take credit for the blight and ruin in their cities, instead blaming the lack of Whites for the collapse of civility and civilization).

We call this "system" Detroit.

Men like Deke Slayton and Michael Collins took for granted that merit was the most valuable way to judge character and competence. In our day, we are forced to push merit aside and judge exclusively by the color of one's skin, as long as we remember: 1) Black is good; 2) White is bad.

The former mindset went to the Moon; the latter mindset enabled the creation of 2014 Detroit.

The collective, individual efforts of hundreds of thousands of White people enabled man to land on the Moon; the collective, individual efforts of hundreds of thousands of Black people enabled Detroit to crumble in its own footprint.

2

About That Black Character in *October Sky*

June 21st, 2014

It's a great movie.

Perhaps one of the best, most motivating movies of the past thirty years.

October Sky.

Homer Hickam.

West Virginia.

The "Rocket Boys."

White boys in 1957, influenced by the Russians launching Sputnik, decide to take up rocketry.

Schools across the country show the movie as part of their curriculum. Homer Hickam's official site even has a study guide to help teachers educate their students on the rocket boys' exploits.

But as in many Hollywood "true stories" (think *Dolphin Tale*), something is incredibly rotten in the state of Denmark when it comes to the inclusion of a Black scientific genius in the city of Coalwood, West Virginia.

A Black scientific genius, who also flew with the Tuskegee Airmen—the "Red Tails"—in World War II.

The character's name in *October Sky* is Leon Bolden. He serves as not only moral support, but technical support as well to the white boys of Coalwood, West Virginia. In fact, here is one of his lines (notice the subtle slip of the "Red Tails" experience into the dialogue):

[A mine worker, formerly one of the Tuskegee Airmen, almost gets hit when he watches Homer launch a rocket]
Leon Bolden: Homer, I flew with the Red Tails in World War II. And seein' that rocket come at me . . . it almost took me back there.

Only problem: there was no Black guy in Coalwood, West Virginia who also flew with the Tuskegee Airmen in World War II, and provided the scientific genius to get the Rocket Boys' experiments off the ground.

There was a White man named Bill Bolt, though:

Bill Bolt doesn't fashion any more nozzles to fuel the dreams of the Rocket Boys.

But he does fashion himself, almost daily, as an informal tour guide for Coalwood. Bolt greets any and all camera-clicking cruisers, orbiting through the wilds of West Virginia and landing here, reaching for the remnants of a proud people, the words of a teacher and the dreams of boys.

"You wouldn't believe the visitors we get," said Bolt, a retired machine shop foreman. "And we still have a lot of people."

Travelers to Coalwood, W.Va., yearn for the nostalgia of the 1950s, when Coalwood's "Rocket Boys" dared to dream beyond the dark and deadly challenges of working in a coal mine.

These "Rocket Boys"—six teenagers who built and launched model rockets—included Homer H. "Sonny" Hickam Jr., a retired NASA engineer who wrote a best-selling memoir called "Rocket Boys" and, by 1999, adapted the book into a big-screen movie, "October Sky."

"Before 'October Sky' came out, we didn't have nothing," said 90-year-old Coalwood resident Red Carroll. "That movie has put us on the map."

In the late 1990s, Hickam won major attention for writing "The Big Creek Missile Agency," a 2,000-word article for Smithsonian Air and Space magazine. Detailing the adventures of his rocket-launching buddies at Big Creek High

School, this piece received so much response that Hickam was inspired to write the "Rocket Boys" book, published in 1998.

Using poetic license, Hickam combined a few characters and used different names for others.

Next came Hollywood, and the movie "October Sky" changed Coalwood even more.

"The movie is about 90 percent true," Bolt figured.

There's a character based on Bolt, but it doesn't look much like him: Actor Randy Stripling, an African-American, portrays a machinist named "Leon Bolden."

Such a switch did not fit reality in Coalwood, Red Carroll said. "There were no black men working in the machine shop."[7]

No Black people in Coalwood, but through the magic of celluloid, you get the numinous Negro.

A magical, technologically, morally superior negro.

Who flew with the Tuskegee Airmen.

Leon Bolden.

Who could only exist via the magic of Hollywood.

Thus, the movie *October Sky* helps show a new generation of "Americans" that only through the contributions of "Red Tails" could white boys from Coalwood, West Virginia find the scientific means to put rockets into the air.

---

[7] Tennis, "Banking on Memories."

3

With NASA's Minority University Research and Education Project (MUREP), Who Needs the Russians to Get to Space?

June 9th, 2014

Ever see the movie *October Sky?*

The true story about four White boys from West Virginia, who take up an interest in rocketry after the Russians successfully launch Sputnik, *October Sky* is a modern classic.

Set in a coal mining town, the main character, Homer Hickam, is portrayed by Jake Gyllenhaal. His father is the mine superintendent.

Easily the most poignant scene occurs after Hickam's father is hospitalized following a mining injury, and Homer must quit school (abandoning his dream of entering his rocket experiments in the science fair and earning a college scholarship) and head down to the mines.

Taking his father's place to become the breadwinner of the family.

As he descends the elevator shaft and into the mine for the first time, Hickam looks up at the night sky at the billions of stars staring just as coldly back at him.

Though his dream would be one day realized, at that moment you feel the dread he did going into the mine.

Leaving a world full of hope and endless possibilities for a dreary, dangerous, and inevitably fatal life of mining coal.

Though we all lead mortal lives, it's the manner in which we live that ultimately gives them meaning and inspires others to greatness.

But that was a different nation.

This is a much different country, whose goal isn't to invest money into projects inevitably taking us to the heavens, but one dedicated to the proposition that a race to the bottom is inherently noble, without contest or debate.

You see, America was a country whose future was quite similar to Homer Hickman's, as he looked at the stars and simultaneously descended into the mineshaft.

Well, the historic majority population is getting the shaft, as we get pulled back down to earth for daring to have the audacity to reach for the stars.

Nothing quite articulates the tragedy of the situation of quite like NASA's *Wings in Orbit: Scientific and Engineering Legacies of the Space Shuttle*, complete with an Orwellian chapter titled "Social, Cultural, and Educational Legacies." It includes subheadings such as "NASA Reflects America's Changing Opportunities" and "NASA Impacts US Culture." On pages 461–462, we inadvertently get a lesson on a period when America looked at the stars knowing they were our potential destination, contrasted against today, when we head into the cold, dark mines of nothingness.

At least we're inclusive, though:

Before the Space Shuttle was conceived, the aerospace industry, NASA employees, and university researchers worked furiously on early human spaceflight programs to achieve President John Kennedy's goal of landing a man on the moon by the end of the 1960s. Although these programs employed thousands of personnel across the United States, White men overwhelmingly composed the aerospace field at that time, and very few women and minorities worked as engineers or scientists on this project.

When they did work at one of NASA's centers, women overwhelmingly served in clerical positions and minorities accepted low-paying, menial jobs.

Few held management or professional positions, and none were in the Astronaut Corps, even though four women had applied for the 1965 astronaut class. By the end of the decade, NASA offered few positions to qualified minorities and women. Only eight Blacks at Marshall Space Flight Center in Alabama held professional-rated positions while the Manned Spacecraft Center (currently known as Johnson Space Center) in Texas had 21, and Kennedy Space Center in Florida had only five.

Signs of change appeared on the horizon as federal legislation addressed many of the inequalities faced by women and minorities in the workplace. During the Kennedy years, the president ordered the chairman of the US Civil Service Commission to ensure the federal government offered positions not on the basis of sex but, rather, on merit. Later, he signed into law the Equal Pay Act of 1963, making it illegal for employers to pay women lower wages than those paid to men for doing the same work. President Lyndon Johnson signed the Civil Rights Act of 1964, which prohibited employment discrimination (hiring, promoting, or firing) on the basis of race, sex, color, religion, or national origin.

Title VII of the Act established the Equal Employment Opportunity Commission, which executed the law. The Equal Employment Opportunity Act of 1972 strengthened the commission and expanded its jurisdiction to local, state, and federal governments during President Richard Nixon's administration. The law also required federal agencies to implement affirmative action programs to address issues of inequality in hiring and promotion practices.

One year earlier, NASA appointed Ruth Bates Harris as director of Equal Employment Opportunity. In the fall of 1973, Harris proclaimed NASA's equal employment opportunity program "a near-total failure." Among other things, the agency's record on recruiting and hiring women and minorities was inadequate. In October, NASA Administrator

James Fletcher fired Harris and Congress held hearings to investigate the agency's affirmative action programs.

Legislators concluded that NASA had a pattern of discriminating against women and minorities. Eventually, a resolution was reached, with Fletcher reinstating Harris as NASA's deputy assistant administrator for community and human relations. From 1974 through 1992, Dr. Harriett Jenkins, the new chief of affirmative action at NASA, began the process of slowly diversifying NASA's workforce and increasing the number of female and minority candidates.[8]

That slow process of diversifying NASA's workforce turned one of the only functional federal agencies into just another US Postal Service, a veritable job program for otherwise unemployable minorities.

But it effectively grounded the ambitions of White men like Homer Hickam, whose aiming for the stars lacked the thrust and power of the diversity craze/initiative.

With NASA now nothing more than a glorified US Postal Service, let's bring up its Minority University Research and Education Program (MUREP).

MUREP is the feel-good program for those who believe one day the racial gap in achievement will be closed and we'll fly to the Moon with just the endless power supplied by our minds.

No rockets.

Just the mind manipulating matter, willing objects into space!

NASA has selected 13 undergraduate teams from minority-serving institutions across the United States to test their science experiments in microgravity conditions. The teams will travel on a Reduced Gravity Education Flight (RGEF) with NASA's Minority University Research and Education Project (MUREP) the week of July 7.

---

[8] NASA, *Wings in Orbit*, 459–69.

Each team designs, flies and evaluates a reduced-gravity experiment that aims to fill technology needs and knowledge gaps previously identified by NASA. They will test their experiments aboard a specially modified aircraft able to simulate a reduced-gravity environment. The aircraft flies approximately 30 sets of rollercoaster-like climbs and dives, producing periods of near weightlessness and hypergravity ranging from 0 to 2 g's. "We are excited that our program provides a once-in-a-lifetime opportunity for aspiring scientists and engineers to study and understand their craft. By participating in this innovative program, the students gain useful skills through collaborative planning and teamwork," said Frank Prochaska, RGEF program manager at NASA's Johnson Space Center in Houston.

The 2014 MUREP teams are from Austin Community College, Austin, Texas; California State Polytechnic University, Pomona; Dallas County Community College District, Dallas; Gadsden State Community College, Gadsden, Alabama; San Jose State University, San Jose, California; Texas Southern University, Houston; University of North Carolina at Pembroke and Robeson Community College, Pembroke, North Carolina; University of Houston; University of Miami, Coral Gables, Florida; University of Puerto Rico at Rio Piedras, San Juan, Puerto Rico; University of Southern California, Los Angeles; University of Texas at El Paso; and, University of Texas Pan American in Edinburg.

MUREP is committed to the recruitment of underrepresented and underserved students in science, technology, engineering and mathematics to sustain a diverse workforce. Participation in NASA projects and research stimulates students to continue their studies at all levels of higher education and earn advanced degrees in these critical fields.[9]

What does "all of the" mean? It's a reminder that as diversity became the goal of NASA, the agency lost its founding focus,

---

[9] NASA, "NASA Selects Minority University Teams."

evolving into just another inefficient federal agency, costly and unproductive.

With more diversity the goal, and press releases congratulating the allocation of money to non-White causes as a reason to celebrate (and exist).

As hostilities with Russia rise again, heating up a Cold War long ago thawed (talk about mixed metaphors), it's important we understand why American astronauts being banned from hitching a ride on Russian rockets is a fitting conclusion to the space race.[10]

It's right there in front of you, if you just open your eyes long enough and embrace the stinging reality of a sun, which long ago set on the American Dream.

As NASA's chief mission became just another self-congratulatory experiment in diversity-hiring and minority-promoting, its history of achievement prior to this new mission statement became an embarrassing reminder of the future Homer Hickman once dreamed of for this country. To those pulling the strings of power in America today, NASA's MUREP program is just as big an achievement as landing on the Moon.

---

[10] Smith, "Russia Bans U.S."

4

1972—The Year NASA's Mandate Changed from
Exploring the Stars to Promoting Affirmative
Action, Diversity, and Equality

May 18th, 2014

The NASA Office of Diversity and Equal Opportunity
(ODEO) represent the great impediment to the next step in human evolution.

It hinders our adventures in space exploration and scientific
advancement, precisely because this office works to handicap
NASA with color-conscious hiring instead of merit-based hiring.

Man's dreams of reaching the stars are grounded, until man
can understand racial differences in intelligence explain the
enormous gap in achievement between Black and White.

On the ODEO website nests this quote, from current NASA
Administrator Charles F. Bolden:

> Journeying beyond Earth's orbit, as NASA is committed to
> do, will require a diverse team of many individuals with the
> best minds, the most comprehensive expertise, the broadest
> knowledge, the strongest talent, and the greatest integrity.
> As NASA's Diversity and Inclusion Champion, I believe it is
> incumbent on every member of the NASA community to ad-
> vocate for, promote, and most importantly, practice the prin-
> ciples of diversity and inclusion in everything that we do.
> This means making diversity and inclusion integral in our
> efforts to identify and develop the best talent, create and

serve on high-performing teams, achieve scientific and engineering excellence, maintain integrity in all that we do, and ultimately, realize mission success.

Unfortunately, Bolden's statement lacks historical veracity.

Sure, he might be NASA's chief Diversity and Inclusion Champion (undisputed champion, mind you), but this position is equivalent to being a greeter at your local Walmart.

His job is to welcome a diverse workforce into an agency that long ago abandoned its mission for space exploration, just as Sam Walton's company long ago abandoned being an American company.

J. Alfred Phelps' book *They Had a Dream: The Story of African American Astronauts* inadvertently provides a key to unlocking a door few people will ever open, instinctively knowing it will only lead them down a rabbit hole the state has spent their entire lives trying to explain doesn't exist.

Racial differences are real.

The state has spent decades and trillions trying to convince you racial differences don't exist, that equality is reality. But don't worry, racial differences believe in you.

Coincidentally, the last manned mission to the Moon was Apollo 17.

This occurred in late 1972.

It represents the last time humans traveled beyond low Earth orbit.

Almost forty-two years ago.

What happened that same year, which could be the unexplained reason behind the end of both space exploration, as well as a powerful rebuttal to Bolden's claim "diversity" will get us to the stars?

The passage of the Equal Employment Act of 1972 and the end of merit hiring at NASA, with the new goal "diversifying" the almost entirely white workforce of the space agency with minorities (and women).

J. Alfred Phelps writes:

With President Lyndon B. Johnson's affirmative action executive order following hard on the heels of the 1964 Civil
Rights Act, and the subsequent passage of the Equal Employment Act of 1972, NASA was forced to give serious consideration to minority hiring.

On September 12th 1973, the NASA Manned Spaceflight
Management Council met in Washington, D.C. Dr. Dudley
G. G. McConnell, the assistant administrator for equal opportunity programs, outlined the chief objectives: Discrimination within NASA must be removed in both fact and ap-
pearance. The new policy targeted all programs and functions. Managers were instructed to support the planning,
implementation, control, and evaluation of the equal opportunity program at every level in the agency, and to verify
that established goals were met.

An Equal Opportunity Action Plan was unveiled. The
plan listed the key elements for Equal Employment Opportunity (EEO) staffing and training. It also provided detailed
goals, time tables, and methods for measuring performance
against the plan. The plan further projected by the end-of-
year numerical goals and wage categories for minority hiring through calendar 1977.

Establishment of an equal opportunity program advisory
board was also directed. Its goal: helping NASA assess the
programs and methods used to attract top minority and female applicants. The board was also tasked to look at "allo-
cating the adverse impact" of certain existing Civil Service
regulations.

Finally, a complete review of functions and planned
membership in a NASA-wide equal opportunity council was
planned. Affirmative action goals for the Kennedy Space
Center (KSC) space-shuttle launch and landing facilities
construction work force were being coordinated to ensure
that minority workers available in the KSC area were being
used.

With those actions, NASA began an astounding turna-
bout in its treatment of women and minorities—its start
fueled by the scrawl of the president's pen.

By February 1974, equal opportunity program meetings at NASA were lively affairs, with open and candid discussions among participants. Equality of involvement was called for in discussions about the recruitment of women and minorities. Greater involvement of middle managers and supervisors in the affirmative action mix was also encouraged.

As defined in 1974, the effort would not only be evident in flight activities, but throughout the NASA work force. Supervisory staff members were directed to attend space centers' human rights seminar, conducted by the Employment Opportunity Office. Each directorate was ordered to develop an affirmative action plan and select a responsible individual authorized to speak on behalf of his organization in "developing and implementing [these] plans." At the Goddard Spaceflight Center, meetings were opened by stressing that "the key word is equality—equality because it is right."[11]

"The key word is equality—equality because it is right."

Does one sentence not elucidate America under the iron heel of the concept of Black-Run America (BRA)?

We went to the Moon with the slide rule; not even with supercomputers and an entire generation held to only one standard and goal—the uplifting of Blacks—can we close the racial gap (Ronald Reagan himself dedicated nearly $1 billion to HBCUs in the 1980s to increase STEM facilities and help future Black engineers and scientists).[12]

When the racial gap is closed, we learn it was through cheating (see the Atlanta Public School scandal).[13]

The Apollo missions weren't saddled with the baggage of government-mandated affirmative action hiring or diversity goals, they only were tasked with landing astronauts safely on the Moon and bringing them home.

---

[11] Phelps, *They Had a Dream*, 60–1.
[12] Sullivan, "Trend Studied."
[13] Sailer, "The Atlanta School Scandal."

This is quite clear in the transcripts of an interview with long-time Deputy Assistant Administrator for Equal Opportunity Programs at NASA, Harriet G. Jenkins.

She started in that role in 1974 (and would serve until 1992). In the interview with Jennifer Ross-Nazzal, we learn this:

> Ross-Nazzal: Tell us, once you became AA [Associate Administrator] of EOP [Equal Opportunity Programs], how you decided to go about integrating the agency. Obviously NASA had a very poor record of hiring women and minorities. So what were some of the first steps you decided to take?
>
> Jenkins: Very importantly, Dr. Fletcher had testified before Congress that NASA had not been as sensitive to those matters during the Apollo era when the agency had hired many employees to build up the needed workforce for that endeavor, and he vowed to correct that oversight.

Oversight? Prior to 1972, the goal of NASA was far, far different from its new mantra: "the key word is equality—equality because it is right."

Because of the belief in inequality, White men's footprints are on the Moon; because of the steadfast belief in equality (mandated by every agency of the federal government on down) Black man's footprint is 2014 Detroit.

5

NASA, Collapse, and Income Inequality: A Simple Thought for Tax Day

April 15th, 2014

On this April 15th, 2014, when your Income Taxes are due to the federal government, let's pause for a second and remember how NASA said society would fall:

Few think Western civilization is on the brink of collapse—but it's also doubtful the Romans and Mesopotamians saw their own demise coming either.

If we're to avoid their fate, we'll need policies to reduce economic inequality and preserve natural resources, according to a NASA-funded study that looked at the collapses of previous societies.

"Two important features seem to appear across societies that have collapsed," reads the study. "The stretching of resources due to the strain placed on the ecological carrying capacity and the economic stratification of society into Elites and Masses."

In unequal societies, researchers said, "collapse is difficult to avoid . . . Elites grow and consume too much, resulting in a famine among Commoners that eventually causes the collapse of society."

As limited resources plague the working class, the wealthy, insulated from the problem, "continue consuming unequally" and exacerbate the issue, the study said.[14]

Not too long ago, Michael Bay directed *Armageddon*, a movie that conclusively showed that only White people had produced the means to stave off a meteorite collision with Earth that would revert worldwide civilization to that of Detroit in 2014.

Bay pays homage to the dream of John F. Kennedy, which is that of going to the Moon and having a vision of space exploration to guide our country into the future.

It's worth remembering America had a choice in the late 1960s, early 1970s: continue funding space exploration or fund the proliferation of the Black underclass (and eventually the offspring of illegal immigrants and refugees brought to enrich America).

Dark Side of the Moon: The Magnificent Madness of the American Lunar Quest by Gerard DeGroot is a book that provides a glimpse into the choice America had before it, even before White men stepped foot on the Moon in 1969.

Would we fund space exploration or pour billions—trillions—into trying to trick nature and close the racial gap in achievement (save the ability for Black individuals to dunk a basketball and run a forty-yard-dash a few tenths of a second faster than Whites)?

DeGroot writes:

LBJ would have preferred to cut military expenditure—in particular, what he called "that bitch of war." [Vietnam]

Civil Rights and the Great Society were his programs, more than they were Kennedy's. Cutting them would be like drowning his baby. In any case, a wave of riots in America's inner cities underlined the fact that the problem of America's black population needed urgent attention, not to

---

[14] Brown and National Journal, "Here's How NASA Thinks."

mention piles of money. That left the space program as the most logical target for cuts.

Enthusiasm for NASA was a manifestation of socioeconomic standing. Those in steady jobs were much more likely to support the space program than those on welfare. Blacks were less enthusiastic than whites, high school dropouts less than college graduates. In the early years, even though it was quite clear that rockets were very expensive, space did not have a direct impact upon the disposable income of employed Americans. The cost seemed affordable, since it had not led directly to tax rises. Fifty cents a week was a small price to pay for all that excitement. But for those in poverty, NASA seemed a cruel manifestation of national priorities.

Going to the Moon was, it appeared, more important than education, welfare, health, or housing. On the margins of society, a constant refrain was heard: "If we can send a man to the Moon, why can't our children read?" "For the poor, the Moon shot seems just another stunt," Whitney Young of the National Urban League, commented at the time. "A circus act. A marvelous trick that leaves their poverty untouched. It will cost thirty-five billion dollars to put two men on the Moon. It would take ten billion dollars to lift every poor person in this country above the official poverty standard this year. Something is wrong somewhere."

The space program was a special boon to the South, with its various installations in Huntsville, New Orleans, Cape Canaveral, and Houston. Some people hoped that this would provide the economic regeneration that would inspire a social transformation—the South would leave behind its racist ways and soar into space. But this did not happen. The sophisticated nature of the work demanded a well-educated, highly trained workforce. As late as 1972, little more than 3 percent of the scientists and engineers working for NASA were black. Granted, there was some manual work for those lower down the social ladder, but, when the contraction began during the Johnson years, the effect was profound. Workers who had left the agrarian sector in order to participate in the lunar challenge found themselves thrown on the scrap heap.[15]

Your taxes go to fulfill the hopes of Whitney Young, who believed ten billion dollars could lift every poor person, magically granting them access to the "American Dream."

The America that put men on the Moon was a great country; the America that decided to invest trillions—without any demonstrable return on investment—into uplifting Black people is not a great country.

A rough road still leads to the stars.

Science fiction writers from Jules Verne to Robert Heinlein to Asimov believed mankind's future was that of exploring the heavens; little did they know the people capable of reaching the stars would spend considerable effort and resources moving from a dangerous, majority Black city (or tipping that way) to another town that will inevitably demographically tip the same way.

Underneath the stars, the universe was once ours.

Today, the federal government will use HUD to map your zip code, neighborhood, and community to ensure it has enough Black enrichment.

We could have been on Mars, but our government decided creating mini-Detroits as official policy from sea to shining sea was a more suitable, nobler goal.

Some of us will live to see to the day when such priorities have changed, forever.

Then, and only then, will our noblest collective aspiration revert from uplifting Black people, to once again watching rockets lift to the heavens.

---

[15] DeGroot, *Dark Side of the Moon*, 199–202.

6

"The Harlem Princess" Ruth Bates Harris: The Woman Who Brought Down the White Man's Rockets and Made Minority Uplifting NASA's No. 1 Priority

June 27th, 2014

Just as the story of Captain Ed Dwight will one day make a fantastic movie for promoting both the concept of Black-Run America (BRA) and the perpetual revolution against White America's past, the even more important story of the 1973 firing of NASA's highest ranking Black female will be fodder for a future Academy Award winning movie.

Ruth Bates Harris, who in 1973 was fired from her $32,000-a-year job as Deputy Assistant Administrator for Equal Opportunity for preparing a forty-page report which made the accusation: "NASA's Equal Opportunity Program is a near-total failure."

Her report charged NASA with the following:

[L]ack of commitment to hiring minorities and called for the replacement of Dudley McConnell [a black man] who, as assistant administrator for equal opportunity, was Mrs. Harris' immediate superior at the space flight agency. The Harris report documented that only 5.19 percent of NASA's employes [*sic*] were members of minority groups, compared to 20 percent for the federal government."[16]

---

[16] *Jet Magazine,* November 15, 1973.

Just as Google, Yahoo, and Facebook have been raked over the coals lately for having too few Black people involved with per-haps the only productive sector of the American economy (out-side of JP Morgan futures in their EBT/SNAP portfolio), NASA's most successful years—you know, going to the Moon—were completely devoid of any Black contributions.

The Indianapolis Recorder, a Black newspaper, devoted lots of ink to discussing the sordid tale of Mrs. Harris' firing, noting on the cover of its November 11th, 1973 edition:

> Mrs. Harris and her staff accused the agency of refusing to take the steps necessary to hire more persons in minority groups. The report also noted that NASA's minority employ-ees had increased only from 4.1 percent in June 1966 to 5.1 percent as of June 1973.
>
> The report also noted that the June figure was down from last June, when minority employment at the agency was 5.2 percent.
>
> Supporters of Mrs. Harris contended that she had been discharged because she pressed the agency too much to im-prove its record.
>
> "NASA has failed to progress because it has never made equal opportunity a priority, said the document from Mrs. Harris and her staff, dated Sept. 20."
>
> It also said: "A sound equal opportunity staff was permit-ted to be formed but it has been continuously kept short of resources and under control of insensitive middle manage-ment. Field installation have been required to establish equal opportunity offices, but in cases where they proposed to appoint unqualified uncommitted persons to staff these programs, the objections of the headquarters equal oppor-tunity staff were overruled."
>
> As of June 30 NASA had a total of 27,031 employees, ac-cording to the equal employment report. There were 1,227 blacks, 270 Spanish-Americans, 192 Orientals and 21 Indians.

Not only were Black people few and far to be found at NASA during its greatest moments, the lack of Orientals (Asians) or Indians (not sure if this denotes the "dot" or "feather" variation) will be cause for altering the chronology of the space agency's achievements to a date far beyond July 20th, 1969.

The best breakdown of the horror Ruth Bates Harris uncovered at NASA was described as by Constance Holden—in the pages of *Science*—as follows: "Nonetheless, the overwhelming white male domination of NASA is making it an increasingly conspicuous and embarrassing anomaly among government agencies."[17]

An increasingly conspicuous and embarrassing anomaly among government agencies. Read that again, and remember those words were published in a major, respected scientific journal in 1973.

1973.

Despite an incredibly positive track record, having a culture and workforce characterized by *overwhelming white male domination* in NASA was *making it an increasingly conspicuous and embarrassing anomaly among government agencies.*

Those who still believe the idea of Moon landing on July 20th, 1969, was a monumental hoax—filmed in some Hollywood studio under the directorship of Stanley Kubrick—need to remember the greatest hoax of all-time is the teaching (and legal notion) of racial equality.

Which, of course, birthed "disparate impact."

Let's look at a few more paragraphs from Constance Holden's 1973 article in *Science*:

On 25 October, James Fletcher, administrator of the National Aeronautics and Space Administration, summoned Ruth Bates Harris, deputy assistant administrator for equal opportunity, into his office and fired her. In so doing, Fletcher may have precipitated just the sort of pressure for improving NASA's employment performance with women

---

[17] Holden, "NASA: Sacking of Top."

and minority group members that critics say it has so far managed to resist.

Even granting NASA the best of intentions, it faces special difficulties in increasing its professional female and nonwhite personnel. As an agency strongly preoccupied by its dramatic scientific missions, it has tended to be dominated by scientific and technical rather than administrative types. Almost half the NASA work force is made up of scientists and engineers, but the national manpower pool contains few women and minority members. Only 1 percent of engineers are female, for example, and 3 percent are nonwhite. Critics point out that NASA contractors, who draw from the same pool of talent, have a far better record in equal employment than NASA. But contractors do not operate under the Civil Service constraints, veterans' preference, and periodic reductions in force that characterize the NASA of the 1970s. What's more, the Office of Federal Contract Compliance is a considerably stronger enforcement agent than the Civil Service Commission, which is responsible for seeing that affirmative action is taken within the government.

Just who was this Ruth Bates Harris, dubbed the "Harlem princess"? NASA published a book in 2009 with the title *Societal Impact of Spaceflight*. Chapter 22 carries the title "Racism, Sexism, and Space Ventures: Civil Rights at NASA in the Nixon Era and Beyond" and it serves as nothing more than hagiography of her efforts to re-triangulate NASA's ambition from the heavens and the exploration of the stars, to being an agency dedicated to nothing more than minority uplift:

The woman Fletcher hired was a self-described "Harlem princess" whose first marriage had been to a Tuskegee Airman.

An honors graduate of Florida A&M University, she had gone on to earn an M.B.A with a specialization in personnel and industrial relations from New York University.

What Fletcher called her "distinguished career in human relations" included service as the executive director of the District of Columbia commission in human relations, a civil rights oversight and implementation group. her nine-year tenure at the DC commission began with a successful push to get The Washington Post to stop carrying racially restricted housing ads, and moved on to an increasing variety of housing, community–police relations, and other work. Through several "long hot summers" of racial discontent in the late 1960s, Harris was among those who exercised front-line leadership in restoring peace and stopping (or avoiding) riots.

Because inhabitants of the nation's capital had only gotten the right to vote for local government in 1967, Harris not only became a De-facto affirmative action officer for city government in a majority African-American metropolis, she also learned to work well with the congress and senators of all political persuasions who were the overseers of DC government.[18]

This is a Hollywood blockbuster without any need for liberties taken by a room full of scriptwriters!

Her first marriage was to a Tuskegee Airmen?

Fought against segregation and restrictive covenants?

Appeared *after* the Black riots had burned much of Washington D.C., scaring away almost all the White population in the process, to restore order?

Check, check, and check!

So, what was Harris, before she was fired (and who NASA officials told a senate inquiry in 1974 was "little more than a lobbyist for the cause of minorities and women") really trying to overcome in her position?

An almost all-White NASA had gone to the Moon and was prepared to begin space exploration.

---

[18] Dick and Launius, *Societal Impact of Spaceflight*, 427.

But Ruth Bates Harris, with the federal government granting her a legal blank check to correct the racially incorrect de-
mographics of NASA employees, had designs other than building a bridge to the stars.

She was working toward, as all federal departments eventually would, building a bridge to the middle-class for Black
people otherwise unemployable in the private sector. More
from the *Societal Impact of Space Flight*:

> NASA, then, talked about wanting "the best equal oppor-
> tunity program in the federal government," but using part-
> time and all-white organizations to do it was naïve. NASA
> employed fewer minorities and women than any other
> agency in government. it claimed this was because of its
> elite and expert technical structure, but far from everyone
> at NASA was a rocket scientist. This disparity between
> NASA and other federal agencies also grew even as African-
> American professionals sought out government agencies as
> employers because those agencies also most often obeyed
> federal civil rights laws. NASA's own statistics showed that
> it did as well as private corporations in employing minori-
> ties and women in the technical half of its operations (at 3.5
> percent), but NASA's leaders did not go on to ask why NASA
> employed only 6 percent of racial minorities in the nontech-
> nical half of its operations. People like Harris were about to
> pose such uncomfortable questions.[19]

Though she was fired in 1973, NASA rehired Harris in 1974.
Jet magazine reported the great news with this announcement:

> Social activist Ruth Bates Harris, who was fired from the
> National Aeronautics and Space Administration in Wash-
> ington, D.C., as deputy assistant administrator for equal op-
> portunity programs, returned recently as deputy adminis-
> trator for community and human relations.

---

[19] Ibid., 429.

In her travels, she will be able to promote NASA and attract minority employes *[sic]* and women to join the
agency.[20]

A hero. There are plenty of conspiracies touting how we never
went to the Moon. It was all a hoax.

Yet the proof of why NASA never went farther than the
Moon, never established a base on the lunar surface, nor dared
consider a mission to Mars, is found in Ruth Bates Harris
"Cheshire Cat" smile.

Chapter 22 of *Societal Impact of Space Flight* ends with this
note:

> It was also a period during which an all-male and all-white
> astronaut corps came to exclude too many other Americans.
> NASA's human spaceflight program would have ceased be-
> ing "manned" and become "human" without Ruth Bates
> Harris or her supporters, but it would have taken signifi-
> cantly longer than the 20 years it did take. NASA and Amer-
> ica's space programs would only have been poorer for it, in
> terms of public interest, understanding, and regard. Ruth
> Bates Harris deserves to be remembered as an important
> actor in the social history of the Space age.[21]

We went to the Moon. This was no hoax. Racial equality is the
hoax.

When a Hollywood studio eventually makes this movie, and
the writers go up on stage to garner their Academy Award for
best picture, you can be sure to thank Paul Kersey.

---

[20] *Jet Magazine*, September 20, 1974.
[21] Dick and Launius, *Societal Impact of Spaceflight*, 449.

7

Department Administering EBT/Food Stamps (USDA) Had Budget of $108 Billion in 2013, and NASA Had Budget of $17 Billion

June 3rd, 2014

The Electronic Benefits Transfer (EBT) card will run out.

When one in four Americans rely on food or nutrition assistance, you know the tipping point is approaching with each passing tick of the clock.

We are funding the creation of undeniably alien worlds within the United States of America: cities that are now alien to the founding, White population of this country.

Hostile, even.

Cities whose citizens rely on handouts, funded by White taxpayer money, just to eat.

Just to live.

The budget of the United States Department of Agriculture (USDA), which administers the EBT card (Temporary Assistance for Needy Families, also known as the Food Stamp Program), is $108.9 billion:

The USDA said it is their responsibility to attempt to alter the food choices of Americans since 25 percent receive food aid from government programs.

"With a total outlay of $108.9 billion in FY 2013, food and nutrition assistance accounted for 72 percent of USDA's budget," the announcement said.

"Approximately 1 in 4 Americans participated in at least 1 of the 15 food and nutrition assistance programs at some point during FY 2013, making these programs fundamental to the nutritional well-being of millions of Americans." . . . "These diverse activities share the common goal of improving the nutrition, food security, and health of American consumers," it said.[22]

The $108.9 billion dedicated to the USDA goes to feed the poor. The hungry.

In 2013, NASA had a budget of $17.6 billion.[23] Peaking in 1965, NASA's budget has continuously been gobbled up by the growth of other federal departments.

Most notably food and nutrition assistance.

You already know what happened on July 16th, 1969: simultaneously both the launch of the greatest journey in world history, and the sorriest moment in all of world history.

The former? The launch of the Apollo 11 mission to the Moon, successfully landing on July 20th, 1969.

The latter? Rev. Ralph Abernathy's Poor People's Campaign, aboard a mule-drawn cart, protesting the White man's technological achievement.

At the 1969 Urban League National Conference, President Whitney Young was quoted as calling the Moon landing "another stunt, a circus act."

[M]oon landing demonstrates wrong national priorities. "For the poor imprisoned in urban slums, it seems just another stunt, a circus act, a marvelous trick that leaves their lives unchanged, their despair untouched."[24]

The trajectory of our national priorities changed.

The Moon, the star, the heavens can wait.

---

22 Harrington, "USDA Creating $1.9 Million."
23 Foust, "NASA Facing New Space."
24 "League's New Goal," *Jet Magazine*, August 4, 1969.

Spending billions on EBT, the TANF, the Women Infants and Children (WIC) program, and other forms of food and nu-trition assistance became the national priority.

Rev. Ralph Abernathy won.

On August 5th, 1969, *The Christian Science Monitor* pub-lished an editorial showing how quickly Rev. Abernathy's mule-drawn cart had changed the trajectory of America's fu-ture. Titled "Both Moon and Earth," the editorial is required reading when it comes to understanding why we are the way we "are" in 2014:

> This newspaper has consistently given strong support to the space program, believing it a worth means of forwarding men's knowledge of the universe and expanding men's own capabilities. We have also resolutely opposed the argument that it was also impossible simultaneously to conduct such a space program and move effectively against the great problems here on earth. We believe that the gigantic eco-nomic wealth and scientific know-how of America is suffi-cient to move forward with both of these worthy programs.
>
> But, while opposing those who say that the space pro-gram should be scrapped in favor of earthside projects, we equally oppose the thinking which would let space achieve-ments turn men's attention from what so desperately needs doing at home. Indeed, in term of man's heart and con-science, the solution of earth's problems is the more im-portant.
>
> Just how important these are can be judged from the fact that several large segments of the American population—notably many blacks and the most militant of young white reformers—have apparently felt little satisfaction in Amer-ica's success on the moon. These groups are so bitter over inequities and distortions in American life that they look upon the space program as almost irrelevant, if not actually harmful to their own interests and struggles.
>
> When spokesmen for varying shades of opinion among America's black citizenry, stretching all the way from the

mild moderation of a Roy Wilkins or a Whitney Young to the bitter and revolutionary outlook of an Eldridge Cleaver and a Stokely Carmichael, draw unflattering contrast between what has been done on the moon and what has not been done at home, then it is well for the country to weigh carefully whether its objectives fully are in balance.

It is a sad thing when any large group of Americans, whose hard work at a thousand different points contributed to the success of the country's space triumphs, feel unable to enjoy to the full this moment of national self-congratulation. It will be even worse, if after this tremendous feat, the imbalance of achievement between the moon and the earth remains.

We are convinced that the vast and diverse fallout from the space program has contributed and will contribute to progress for all on earth. This is above all true where men's broadened and heightened outlook on mankind's capabilities are revealed. Once you go to the moon, poverty and inequity on earth seem all the more intolerable. But what is needed right now is proof to America's disaffected that, while the country has one eye on space, it has both its eyes on their many problems.

The EBT Card will run out. This present will default. Our future is not Detroit.

8

NASA's Final Frontier: Finding the Great Black Scientist

December 22nd, 2010

We all know of NASA's current mission, with Muslim outreach now the primary goal of that once vaunted organization.

NASA is attempting to address the "critical" shortage of Black people within the ranks of science and engineering fields, at a time when many high schools are doing away with honors programs and gifted classes because of a shortage of Black people in their ranks. With fewer Black students taking AP exams (and fewer garnering a three or above), one is left wondering where NASA will locate potential Black astrobiologists.

Curbing excellence seems to be a ploy to remove all remnants of White people excelling where Black people constantly fail. Perhaps if science labs are removed from high schools (as in Berkeley), the stunning athletic achievements of Black people will somehow progress our levels of scientific knowledge.

Instead of investing money in the "gifted" segments of society, we are intent on devesting those programs and redistributing that money to areas of consistent failure:

> NASA has selected the United Negro College Fund Special Programs Corp. of Falls Church, Va., to administer a $1 million career development and educational program designed to address the critical shortage of U.S. minority students in science and engineering fields.

The NASA Astrobiology Institute's (NAI) Minority Institution Research Support (MIRS) program in Moffett Field, Calif., is providing the funding for the four-year effort. The program will provide opportunities for up to four faculty members and eight students from minority-serving institutions to partner with astrobiology investigators. Astrobiology is the study of the origin, evolution, distribution and the future of life on Earth and the potential for life elsewhere.

"Providing new education opportunities for minority students will both enrich lives and answer a critical need for proficiency in science and engineering," NASA Administrator Charles Bolden said. "But just as importantly, the program is an investment to cultivate imaginative thinking about the field of astrobiology."

The United Negro College Fund Special Programs Corp. will use its extensive database of 14,000 registrants to develop an online community to provide webinars, virtual training and videoconferences, and provide outreach and recruitment for program participants. The program's objective is to engage more teachers from under-represented schools in astrobiology research and increase the number of students pursuing careers in astrobiology.

"Our nation's underserved populations are a tremendous resource on which we must draw, not just for science, but for everything we do," said Carl Pilcher, director of NASA's Astrobiology Institute. "We are extremely pleased that the NAI MIRS program will continue contributing under the leadership of such a strong and experienced partner."

Founded in 1998, NAI is a partnership between NASA, 14 U.S. teams of universities and other organizations, and seven international consortia. NAI's goals are to promote, conduct, and lead interdisciplinary astrobiology research, train a new generation of astrobiology researchers, and share the excitement of the field.[25]

---

[25] NASA, "NASA Awards $17.6 Million."

One of the first rules of Stuff Black People Don't Like is that any organization that fails to have significant numbers of Black people (or vocational fields) is operating at crisis level. Only with the introduction of large numbers of Black people can offset this horrible situation, for the efficiency of an organization and its status as a progressive, tolerant company (or vocation) is at stake.

So how many Black astrobiologists are there?

During the Astrobiology Science Conference held at NASA Ames in April 2002, less than 1% of the 800 attendees were African-American. To increase the visibility and participation of underrepresented scientists, The Minority Institution Astrobiology Collaboratory (MIAC) was formed.[26]

A sane society would have no problem asking why that might be, but an insane society merely enquires as to how a greater representation of Black people will be possible (hint: lowering standards in becoming an astrobiologist).

One institution that has allocated money for NASA, and is a predominately Black university, is Alabama Agricultural & Mechanical (Alabama A&M). A top producer of Black people with advanced doctorates, Alabama A&M is also home to growing controversy that involves NASA, tens of millions of dollars, and a chief compliance officer who used to be a janitor:

According to high ranking officials at Alabama A&M University, the FBI has started asking questions about recent events at the Research Institute.

That's the flagship scientific research program, an 11-year-old separate corporate entity that employs A&M professors to handle millions in private and government research contracts on behalf of NASA, the Defense Department and numerous companies, such as Boeing.

---

[26] MIAC, "Main Pages."

"Yes, some senior administrators have been informed of a potential situation with the Research Institute," said university spokesperson Wendy Kobler on Thursday when asked about the FBI investigation. "Of late, there have been no follow up conversations about the ongoing inquiry into the Research Institute."

According to the former institute attorney, Annary Cheatham, after a summer of more than five firings and forceouts, there's just about no one left at the institute with a background in science or with the necessary security clearance.

The institute's small governing board, which includes former A&M trustee Shefton Riggins and current A&M trustee Tom Bell, on June 14 held a private meeting and fired the man who had helped found the institute, physicist and longtime director Dr. Daryush Ila.

They hired Dr. Tommy Coleman, who has a background in plant and soil science. In July, the board removed Coleman and put in director Deidra Willis-Gopher, a former teacher.

Kevin Matthews, a former Madison County janitor, became the new chief compliance officer. And Cheatham, who was brought in as general counsel for the institute on July 20 and let go 15 days later, said the bylaws were rewritten to place Matthews on the Institute board with Riggins and Bell, meaning Matthews is, in part, supervising himself.[27]

Yes, the chief compliance officer that oversaw millions in grants was a former janitor.

Like all government agencies, NASA exceeds its employment of Black people, correlated to the percentage of the overall US population, by 49 percent.[28] This isn't enough, as NASA lags in diversity:

---

[27] Stephens, "FBI Asking Questions." Emphasis mine.
[28] Adversity, "2007 Edition."

In a year of firsts, the nomination of an African-American to lead NASA hasn't grabbed national front-page headlines used for a black president moving into the White House, or for the selection of a Hispanic justice for the U.S. Supreme Court.

Yet, if former astronaut Charles Bolden is confirmed as the next NASA administrator, he will take over an agency still struggling to match the racial diversity found in the nation's population, much less the federal work force in general.

Part of the reason is because minorities are underrepresented in the science-and-math-related professions from which NASA draws, said space policy expert Howard McCurdy.

But that doesn't excuse NASA, he said.

"The federal government has viewed itself as having a special responsibility to be a model employer, to go beyond what the occupational distribution allows," said McCurdy, a public affairs professor at American University in Washington, D.C.

"I don't sense that NASA moves much beyond what the occupational categories provide them. They are much more comfortable with technical challenges than with social ones."

When it comes to racial parity, NASA falls short in all but one ethnic group, Asian-Americans. At Kennedy Space Center, the situation is a little different.

Blacks, who make up 12.8 percent of the U.S. population, represent 11.3 percent of NASA's employees. They make up 17.9 percent of the federal work force. At KSC, blacks make up 7.6 percent of the work force, compared with 10 percent of Brevard County's population.

Hispanics represent 5.9 percent of all NASA employees, although they make up 7.9 percent of the federal labor force and 15.1 percent of the nation's population. Ten percent of KSC's work force is made up of Hispanics, compared with 6.9 percent of Brevard's population.

Asian-Americans, who make up 4.6 percent of the national population, represent 6.3 percent of NASA's work force. That's nearly double the 3.4 percent they represent of all government employees. At KSC, 4.2 percent of the work force is made up of Asian-Americans, compared with 2.1 percent of Brevard's population."[29]

We once went to the Moon. We can't go back now, not because mankind is getting dumber, but because mankind must curb excellence so that Black people won't be left out. Honors classes, military entrance exams, AP exams, the SAT, LSAT, MCAT and ACT, the Wonderlic and any other test that requires a No. 2 pencil must go, because they deny Black people the opportunity to bless many vocations with wondrous variety and diversity.

American innovation has been handicapped by the failures of Black people and to compensate for this continued poor academic showing (and thus high rate of barber shop employees), all companies or organizations—both public and private—must lower standards.

To understand why America made it to the Moon in 1969 is to understand where America would be ranked in the PISA scores internationally were the White score not saddled with those of an underachieving racial group.

The contributions of Black people cannot go unnoticed: where would the world be without the Super Soaker or this nifty invention to hold up sagging pants?

We need only look to modern Huntsville to see where mankind is heading, thanks to Antoine Dodson.

Those of us looking at the year 2010 coming to a close realize the world of *Harrison Bergeron* is upon us.

---

[29] Daily Kos, "On Diversity, NASA Lags Behind. New Poll."

9

Dumb and Dumber: The Future of NASA

July 6th, 2010

News of space exploration being halted on the grounds of insufficient outreach to Muslim nations has been greeted with incredulity by most normal people:

NASA Administrator Charles Bolden said in a recent interview that his "foremost" mission as the head of America's space exploration agency is to improve relations with the Muslim world. Bolden said in an interview with Al Jazeera that strengthening those ties was among the top tasks President Obama assigned him. He said better interaction with the Muslim world would ultimately advance space travel.

"When I became the NASA administrator—or before I became the NASA administrator—he charged me with three things. One was he wanted me to help re-inspire children to want to get into science and math, he wanted me to expand our international relationships, and third, and perhaps foremost, he wanted me to find a way to reach out to the Muslim world and engage much more with dominantly Muslim nations to help them feel good about their historic contribution to science . . . and math and engineering," Bolden said in the interview.

The NASA administrator was in the Middle East last month marking the one-year anniversary since Obama delivered an address to Muslim nations in Cairo. Bolden spoke in June at the American University in Cairo—in his interview with Al Jazeera, he described space travel as an international collaboration of which Muslim nations must be a part.

"It is a matter of trying to reach out and get the best of all worlds, if you will, and there is much to be gained by drawing in the contributions that are possible from the Muslim (nations)," he said. He held up the International Space Station as a model, praising the contributions there from the Russians and the Chinese.[30]

Thankfully, African nations are leading the push into space. The website "First African in Space" details the exploits of an astronaut that penetrated earth's atmosphere for low orbit in 2002. However, upon examination of the website, incontrovertible proof is provided that the first African in space was of non-African descent.

Thankfully, the new South Africa is investing money into a space program that has the mission of actually exploring space, as opposed to Muslim outreach. Nigeria and other African nations are also replacing the United States' role as the creative force behind carrying mankind's hopes and dreams into space.

And who can forget Uganda's president declaring the intentions of that nation—to penetrate the endless abyss of space?

Africans must travel to the moon to investigate what developed nations have been doing in outer space, Ugandan President Yoweri Museveni said Saturday.

"The Americans have gone to the moon. And the Russians. The Chinese and Indians will go there soon. Africans are the only ones who are stuck here," Museveni said, addressing a meeting of the Uganda Law Society in Entebbe.

"We must also go there and say: 'What are you people doing up here?'"

---

[30] Fox News, "NASA Chief: Next Frontier."

Museveni urged the assembly of Uganda's top lawyers to support East African integration, arguing that one of the region's goals should be to develop a space programme.

"Uganda alone cannot go to the moon. We are too small. But East Africa united can. That is what East African integration is all about," he said. "Then we can say to the Americans: 'What are you doing here all alone?'"

Museveni has vocally campaigned for a common East African economic and political zone.

Negotiations to establish a tariff free trade zone including Uganda, Kenya, Tanzania, Burundi and Rwanda have been ongoing for months.

Museveni on Saturday also called for enhanced political integration among the East African nations, suggesting the region would be strengthened by becoming one country.[31]

Apollo 13 and *The Right Stuff* are both movies that glorify pre-Obama America and a people who once had the audacity to travel to the Moon. That audacious and fearless attitude is now best directed toward helping propel the self-esteem of Muslim nations skyward, helping them dream big, and uplifting every Mohammedan heart.

The future of NASA is to be relegated to the punch line from the film *Dumb and Dumber*, when Lloyd Christmas finds out, rather belatedly, that we landed on the Moon.

The achievements of NASA occurred at a time of profound Whiteness—an embarrassing fact to Black-Run America—and thus all energy and efforts of the interstellar government agency have been grounded by a most terrestrial goal.

The 1996 movie *Independence Day*—perhaps the most politically incorrect movie ever made—has an interesting montage scene at the end where the alien ships have been downed in a global aerial battle, the world's citizens emerging victorious. In one scene, scurrying from the jungle, are African males carrying spears and raising them triumphantly, celebrating

---

[31] Museveni, "Africans must travel to the moon."

the destroyed alien ship that utilized a gravitational device to hover in the air miles above the ground.

It would be foolish to believe any arm could contain the power to throw a spear the required distance to bring ruin to the spaceship, but somehow the absurdity of the scene managed to withstand editing and found its way into the finished version of the film.

This one scene epitomizes the vast differences that exist in humanity, as the valley in human biodiversity is a wide gulf that no amount of wishing will ever bridge.

NASA's grandest accomplishment, sending a man to the Moon, is of little concern anymore and will be excised from future textbooks giving way to the true final frontier facing man: helping out the Muslim world.

Dumb and Dumber indeed.

Then again, NASA was always a pitiable waste of money. The billions, trillion (perhaps quadrillions) spent on space travel would have been better spent on earthly endeavors, perhaps uplifting the poor and wretched.[32]

The desire since time immemorial to travel into space and traverse the unknown has been a driving force behind the creative minds of the top civilizations that have arisen on earth. Though they may have fallen, new civilizations arose with aspirations of exploring the heavens.

Finally, those dreams came to fruition when a people decided to sever the roots that had held mankind to the ground so harshly for centuries. On July 20th, 1969, a date which commemorates the culmination of that people's ingenuity, a man stepped onto the Moon and came in peace for all mankind.

The apex of space travel was achieved nearly forty-one years ago. Now, the ambitions of a distinct people have been tied down, chained to the people of earth who never resolved to lose those terrestrial ropes in the first place.

---

[32] DeGroot, "The Space Race Is a Pointless."

People will forget that we ever went to the Moon, as Lloyd Christmas shows but a glimpse of the future in the aforementioned movie.

10

Debunking the Moon Landing Hoax: In 1970, Blacks Throughout America Expressed Disbelief Whitey Could Have Made It to the Moon

June 17th, 2014

There's one thing that's always bothered me: those who claim we never went to the Moon.

The belief in the "we never went to the Moon" conspiracy represents the repudiation of *our* civilization, for it was White men from the nations of Europe who labored in the quest to make that "one giant leap for mankind" possible; just as it was exclusively Black people who labored in the quest to remake cities like Detroit, Memphis, and Philadelphia in their image.

Germans.

Russians.

Englishmen.

Scots.

Irish.

Danes.

Swedes.

French.

Albion's seed here in America.

In what amounts to a mere blink of an eye in the grand scheme of human history, men pushed the boundaries of known science and not only achieved mastery of rocketry, but also established NASA as the foremost example of effective bureaucracy in the history of human resource management.

Well, until the destination for NASA became not the stars, but just another federal agency dedicated to affirmative action and minority hiring in 1972.

So, it should come as no surprise much of the initial skepticism for the successful Apollo 11 mission came from a community whose greatest achievement is the complete dismantling of the civilization Whites created in neighborhoods and cities throughout this country: the Black community.

Yes, immediately upon landing on the Moon, Blacks from Chicago to Harlem, from Macon to Washington, D.C., found incredulous the story of three White men traveling more than a hundred thousand miles and back, when their community was incapable of keeping a simple laundry mat open:

How widespread were the sceptics about the Moon landings in the 1960s? That is almost impossible to say. For example, New York Times science reporter John Noble Wilford remarked in December 1969 that a few stool- warmers in Chicago bars are on record as suggesting that the Apollo 11 moonwalk last July was actually staged by Hollywood on a Nevada desert. More important, the Atlanta Constitution led a story on June 15, 1970, with: Many skeptics feel moon explorer Neil Armstrong took his giant step for mankind' somewhere in Arizona.

It based its conclusion that an unspecified-many questioned the Apollo 11 and 12 landings, and presumably the April 1970 accident aboard Apollo 13, on an admittedly unscientific poll conducted by the Knight Newspapers of 1,721 U.S. citizens in Miami, Philadelphia, Akron, Ohio, Detroit, Washington, Macon, Ga., and several rural communities in North and South Carolina. Those polled were asked—do you really, completely believe that the United States has actually landed men on the moon and returned them to earth again?

While numbers questioning the Moon landing in Detroit, Miami, and Akron averaged less than five percent, among African Americans in such places as Washington, D.C., a whopping 54 percent doubted the moon voyage had taken place. That perhaps said more about the disconnectedness of minority communities from the Apollo effort and the na-tion's overarching racism than anything else. As the story reported, a woman in Macon said she knows she couldn't watch a telecast from the moon because her set wouldn't even pick up New York stations.[33]

When the individual contributions of members of your commu-nity create poverty, crime, and misery, how can you view the collective achievement of White individuals as anything other than a hoax, unless you're willing to admit the inherent inferi-ority of not only your community, but also the individuals who call it home?

If the Moon landing can be brushed off as a hoax or a con-spiracy, a member of the Black community is thus able to ra-tionalize the complete failure of their race's ability to assimi-late to the American Dream, due to the gross misuse of public funds on the elaborate Apollo ruse.

After all, we're all equal:

But when Knight Newspapers (one of the two groups that later merged to form Knight-Ridder Inc.) polled 1,721 US residents one year after the first moon landing, it found that more than 30 percent of respondents were suspicious of NASA's trips to the moon. A July 20, 1970, *Newsweek* arti-cle reporting the results of the poll cited "an elderly Phila-delphia woman who thought the moon landing had been staged in an Arizona desert" and a Macon, Georgia, house-wife who questioned how a TV set that couldn't pull in New York stations could possibly "receive signals from the moon." The greatest skepticism, according to *Newsweek*, surfaced in a ghetto in Washington, DC, where more than half of those interviewed doubted the authenticity of Neil Armstrong's stroll. "It's all a deliberate effort to mask

---

[33] Launius, "Denying the Apollo Moon Landings."

problems at home," explained one inner-city preacher. "The people are unhappy—and this takes their minds off their problems."[34]

The most flagrant hoax of our time is that of racial equality, for it allows the continued allocation of precious resources—White taxpayer money—to try and close whatever racial gap exists in learning, achievement, or fire fighter scores.

It allows for the business and corporate back-breaking ruling of disparate impact to handicap and retard any competitive advantage garnered by a lack of Black employees within an organization (US Postal Service in 2014 vs. NASA pre-1972).

So go ahead and believe we never went to the Moon.

There's more evidence we went to the Moon than exists evidence we can ever lift the Black race to the civilizational standards set by Europeans—by Americans.

Our future should have been the stars, yet the world stands on the Malthusian edge because we dared dismantle our civilization to show race didn't exist.

Well, it does.

The Moon landing is proof of this.

Which is why, to the Black community, it must be a hoax.

---

[34] Kaysing, "The Wrong Stuff."

11

Time and *Newsweek* Noticed the Scarce Number of Blacks at
Apollo 11 Moon Launch in Articles Published in 1969

April 24th, 2014

Gary Edgerton's book *The Columbia History of American
Television* offers another fascinating glimpse into the most
striking example of racial differences in recorded history: when
Black people arrived on mule-drawn carts in Cape Canaveral—
as part of the Poor People's March—to protest the Apollo 11
Moon launch.

Part of the *Columbia Histories of Modern American Life*,
Edgerton's work includes quotes from the July 28th, 1969 issue
of *Newsweek* and the July 25th, 1969 issue of *Time*. Both peri-
odicals lament the general Whiteness of the Moon launch:

> On July 16, an estimated "1,000,000 earthlings, a record
> outpouring for a launch, had jammed the beaches near the
> Cape to give Apollo 11 a lusty, shoulder-to-shoulder send off.
> Among the gathered multitude were Vice President Spiro T.
> Agnew, Lady Bird and former President Lyndon Johnson,
> Senator Barry Goldwater, Jack Benny, Johnny Carson, 200
> congressmen, 100 foreign ministers, and 275 leaders of com-
> merce and industry. CBS reporter Charles Kuralt observed
> that Americans had gone "moon mad." *Time*, in contrast,
> asked, "Is the moon white?"
>
> "On launch day," the magazine continued, "the VIP
> grandstand was a miniature *Who's Who of white America;*
> it was disturbing to notice that black faces were scarce."

Opposition to the expensive space program was especially strong inside the nation's African American community. "Texas, with its oil wells, large farms, and now space center of the world, symbolizes the affluent America," said Herbert James, the black field director of the National Welfare Rights Organization, "but there exists in this great state a despicable amount of poverty. Starvation and hunger are taking place within miles of the space center."

A "mule-cart procession of the Poor People's March, led by Ralph Abernathy," also arrived to protest the Moon launch on July 16. When the civil rights leaders saw the Apollo 11 liftoff, however, "he forgot about poverty and prayer for the safety of the men." At least temporarily, the Moon landing generated an unprecedented level of interest in the space program, although some cohorts were clearly more excited by the telecast than others. "If to many the moon seemed white, it also seemed middle-aged," *Time* further surmised; "the young, who have grown up in the TV and space age, seemed the most blasé of all.[35]

Time magazine wrote it was "disturbing to notice that Black faces were scarce" at the launch of the Apollo 11, despite that outside of Black custodians employed by NASA, there were few Blacks involved in the space program.

How dare White America get to the Moon without Black involvement!

Well, it was Black involvement in the running of Detroit that brought the once proud city to its knees. Sadly, *Time* or *Newsweek* won't lament the "disturbing" lack of Black faces that were anything but scarce in the destruction of the city.

Luckily, Ze'ev Chafets' 1990 book *Devil's Night: And Other True Tales of Detroit* supplies a quote that helps put into perspective the blight and ruin Detroit has become. In fact, it clearly shows what happens when Black faces are no longer disturbingly scarce.

---

[35] Edgerton, *Columbia History*, 272–3.

It shows what happens when White faces are scarce.

George Crockett, eventual congressman and longtime Black judge in Detroit—during the racial transformation of that city from majority White to majority Black—was a force in antago- nizing the dwindling the White population of the city, and con- vincing them to find new real estate to call home.

Chafets wrote:

> A few days earlier, in a special report on the thirteenth Dis- trict, the local NBC affiliate had called him "George Crock- ett, Third World congressman" – a reference to both his ide- ology and the devastation of his district. Crockett chose to take the reference as a compliment.
>
> "Third World?" he mused. "Well, there's something to that. Detroit is the black capital of the United States. When I first ran for City Council, back in 1965, I predicted that within ten years Detroit would be a majority black city with a black leadership, and I was right. One problem of postcolo- nial societies is a lack of prepared leadership cadres, espe- cially in places like Angola and Mozambique, which were under Portuguese rule. We're not quite that bad, but there's room for comparison.
>
> "We had a white outflow that I'm not aware has been du- plicated in any other metropolitan area in the United States," he continued. "There is urban-suburban animosity because whites lost money in running, and because they still want access to the library, the symphony, the ballpark, and getting to them is inconvenient. So, that way, too, there is room for comparison to a postcolonial situation."[36]

Detroit was colonized. It was 98 percent white 100 years ago and was more than 84 percent white in 1950. Blacks had noth- ing to do with building Detroit, but everything to do with the destruction of Detroit.

---

[36] Chafets, *Devil's Night*, 118–9.

Blacks remade the city in their image, with Whites an increasingly scarce sight in the city. Hell, the currently named GM Renaissance Center was built as a fortress to protect White workers from the increasingly dangerous Black city streets.

Underneath the stars, the universe was once ours. Those writers for *Time* and *Newsweek*, who lamented the overt Whiteness of the Apollo 11 Moon launch in 1969, were part of the tidal wave of opinion that helped ensure the universe became the property of those who remade Detroit in their image.

Blacks.

Those same people who arrived at the July 16th, 1969 Apollo 11 Moon launch riding a horse and buggy. When juxtaposed with the Apollo 11 rocket—the culmination of individual White people's collective will and brainpower—you get a picture of why Detroit became the city it is today, courtesy of Black people's collective will and brainpower.

When four Black males are accused of attacking a White male in 83 percent Black Detroit, and their relatives laugh at their charges, you get a glimpse of the type of community Black people create, and the culture they foster.[37]

When a White immigrant from Australia moves to Detroit to seek his "American Dream" (being a slumlord tenant in an 83 percent Black city is somehow a "dream") and is murdered by one of the Black tenants he is evicting, you learn the true nature of what being the capital of Black America means. One of the people who attacked him—before he was shot to death—stated: "I'm tired of you white people."[38]

A pro-Black, anti-White mindset permeates throughout modern, 83 percent Black Detroit. After all, to quote Crockett, it's "the black capital of America."

Once, it was federal policy for Americans to reach for the stars, to reach for the heavens.

Today, it is federal policy for Americans to regress to the level of 2014 Detroit; instead of reaching for the heavens, to

---

[37] Deadline Detroit, "At Utash Court Hearing."
[38] AAP, "Detroit witness."

stare blankly at the stars while our future becomes increasingly that of the horse-and-buggy piloted by Blacks back in
1969.

Time and *Newsweek* published articles back in July of 1969
lamenting the lack of Black faces watching the greatest
achievement in mankind's history. Well, European history.

No one dared point out the scarcity of White people involved
in the Detroit city government when the Black capital of America was forced to declare bankruptcy in 2013.

12

Happy 50th Birthday Civil Rights Act of 1964

June 23rd, 2014

Fifty years!

Happy Birthday, Civil Rights Act of 1964!

Birthed on June 19th, this act ushered in a new era of legalized discrimination against Whites, all in the name of uplifting the Black population (and now, the Hispanic population is protected via this fifty-year-old legislation).

For a fifty-year-old act, it still looks good, right?

No need for Botox or a tummy tuck, the Civil Rights Act of 1964 gets plenty of exercise on a daily basis.

Fifty years ago, on July 2, 1964, one of the biggest legal barriers to equal opportunity in America was toppled when President Lyndon Johnson signed into law the most sweeping civil rights legislation since the Reconstruction era. The Civil Rights Act of 1964 outlawed discrimination in such areas as voting, public restaurants, employment, and education on the basis of such characteristics as race, color, religion, national origin, and sex. It was a pivotal moment in our nation's struggle to form "a more perfect union" and transformed the face of America.[39]

"Form a more perfect union?"

---

[39] NASA, "NASA Celebrates the 50th Anniversary."

Since the passing of the Civil Rights Act of 1964, how many American cities have become no-go areas for White people?

How many of these formerly American cities are filled not only with crime and blight, but run democratically by a people "liberated" by the 1964 Act?

After World War II, much of Europe was ravaged with burnt out cities; Hiroshima and Nagasaki were atomic wastelands.

What can be said of Birmingham, Memphis, Detroit, Camden, Baltimore, and Newark?

No one will say it, so we will: the Civil Rights Act of 1964 ensured the dissolving of the United States of America and the dismantling of any "more perfect union" talk.

Its passing was far more damaging to the health of the country than any foreign military could hope to replicate.

And yet, we must always praise this fifty-year-old legislation as the pivotal moment in rectifying inequities of our incurable racist past—well, only incurable until the past can be rewritten to find true non-White heroes worthy of our adulation, love, and respect.

New heroes must emerge to lionize and praise as the foundation of our country, since we will one day celebrate the true birth of the nation as June 19th, 1964:

On May 13, 1961, in its first issue after Alan Shepard's historic Mercury mission, the nation's leading black newspaper, the *New York Amsterdam News*, ran a front-page column that asked a question on the minds of millions of Americans. "If you are like me," wrote executive editor James Hicks, "as soon as you finished thrilling to the flight of the United States's first man into outer space, your next thought was, 'I wonder if there were any Negroes who had anything to do with Commander Shepard's flight?'"

There is a short list of steps NASA took to promote equal employment in the year before the 1964 Civil Rights Act became law: The agency created a contractors' group in Alabama that used its money and influence to make sure African-Americans got space jobs. NASA hired Charlie Smoot, called the "first Negro recruiter" in official agency histories, to travel the nation persuading black scientists and engineers to come south. The Marshall Space Flight Center invited representatives of the historically black colleges to Huntsville in 1963, and a year later opened the agency's college cooperative education program—in which students alternated semesters at school with semesters at Marshall—to blacks.

As a result, Walter Applewhite, Wesley Carter, George Bourda, Tommy Dubone, William Winfield, Frank C. Williams Jr., and Morgan Watson arrived at Marshall to become the embodiment of Johnson's plan for jobs in the South.

Space—and Race—Progress

The idea that the Space Age might help usher in better race relations became a subject of scientific inquiry. In the spring of 1962, NASA made a grant to the American Academy of Arts and Sciences to study "the relationships of space efforts to US society." The report proceeded, in part from the popular conception that NASA, in the academy's words, represented "a new era of equality according to ability." There was a belief that "communities with advanced types of industry, with their people employed in research laboratories and in the development of new engineering techniques, should display a high level of social innovation."

The academy sent sociologist Peter Dodd to the space communities to find out if it was true. In multiple visits to Huntsville, Florida's Cape Kennedy, and the Manned Spacecraft Center in Houston, Texas, Dodd spoke to NASA workers and administrators as well as municipal officials, city planners, newspapermen, ministers, educators, social workers, housewives, and teenagers.

Studies suggested that space workers had "high levels of education, which are known to be correlated with liberal views," and that "their youth and geographic mobility have exposed them to liberal opinion." What Dodd found was exactly the opposite, especially in matters of race. In Huntsville and at Cape Kennedy, he said, "There seem to be no evidence of strong pressure for Negro rights, nor of strong sympathy among technologists for civil rights." To NASA workers, he found, "the Negroes appear to be an outside group presenting demands which would have to be dealt with in some way, but which are no concern of theirs."[40]

How dare those White males in NASA not understand the Blacks forced upon them were their moral superiors (and obviously intellectual superiors, which goes without saying).

Talk about your made-for-Hollywood story: praise Black ingenuity (all part of an early affirmative action scheme to scour the country to find suitable Black scientists) while denouncing the racist Whites at NASA, for refusing to accept the notion that merit had no place in the workplace when Blackness was involved.

But it is in Andrew J. Dunar's *Power to Explore: A History of Marshall Space Flight Center, 1960–1990* that we get a clear look at how impactful the 1964 Civil Rights Act was on NASA:

> Attorney General Robert Kennedy, long a critic of Vice President Lyndon B. Johnson's leadership of the President's Committee on Equal Employment Opportunity, met with the committee on 18 June. Webb, a protégé of Johnson, represented NASA. Kennedy grilled Johnson, puncturing his vague claims of progress. After "making the Vice President look like a fraud," in the words of one observer, the Attorney General turned on [James] Webb. "Mr. Webb, I just raised a question of whether you can do this job and run a Center and administer its $3.9 billion worth of contracts and make sure that Negroes and nonwhites have jobs . . . I am trying to ask some questions. I don't think I am able to get the answers, to tell you the truth."
>
> Marshall established an Affirmative Action Program in June, following recommendations offered by a Civil Service team from Atlanta. Dr. Frank R. Albert became the first

---

[40] Paul, "How NASA Joined the Civil Rights Revolution."

Equal Employment Opportunity Coordinator. Albert hired Charlie Smoot as a professional staffing recruiter; Marshall claimed Smoot was "possibly the first Negro recruiter in government service."

Marshall's shortcomings represented a portion of a larger NASA failure. NASA lagged behind other federal agencies in implementing equal opportunity programs. NASA's minority employment rose only from 4.1 percent to 5.19 percent between 1966 and 1973, when overall federal minority employment reached 20 percent. Furthermore, most of its minority employees were clustered in lower grades. The Agency's own EEO staff concluded that "NASA has failed to progress because it has never made equal opportunity a priority." Deputy Administrator George Low conceded that "Equal Opportunity is a sham in NASA," and derided the Agency's "total insensitivity to human rights and human beings."[41]

By 1973, the federal government workforce was 20 percent non-White (primarily Black, considering the demographic explosion of Hispanics and Asians was yet to occur), but NASA was roughly 95 percent white.

Remember: it was in 1972 that NASA became just another federal—taxpayer funded—minority jobs program.

But as the book *Societal Impact of Spaceflight* makes clear, NASA in 1973 did have a place for Blacks: 69 percent of the janitors at NASA were minority (Black) males, compared to a government-wide average of 56 percent!

That's progress.

And, like in the movie *Good Will Hunting*, it was really a Black janitor named Robert Wall who helped break a complex math equation Wernher Von Braun left on a chalkboard for one of NASA's insensitive White nerds to try and solve (true story).

So happy fiftieth birthday, Civil Rights Act of 1964.

---

[41] Dunar and Waring, *Power to Explore*, 124.

It might just be, but when I look at the ruins of a city like Detroit, I don't see the harmful legacy of capitalism or Democrat rule: I see the legacy of the 1964 Civil Rights Act in full glory.

And NASA being turned into just another United States Postal Service—well, that's just another legacy of the 1964 Civil Rights Act.

13

The Wrong Stuff—The Ed Dwight Story: John F. Kennedy's Crusade to Find and Promote a "Negro Astronaut"

May 4th, 2014

Had John F. Kennedy not been assassinated, one of the first men to walk on the Moon might have been a Negro astronaut, deliberately picked by his administration to be part of the astronaut training programming because he was a Black man.

His name was Ed Dwight.

Sure, he had logged flight time and had an aeronautical engineering degree, but Capt. Ed Dwight's primary skillset was being one of the few qualified Black men the Kennedy Administration could quickly promote into the NASA astronaut candidate program.

His black skin qualified him for immediate promotion into the merit-based astronaut-training program that had been exclusively the hunting of White men who had earned their way there.

J. Alfred Phelps book *They Had a Dream: The Story of African American Astronauts,* includes a look at just how aggressive the Kennedy Administration was in promoting a Negro astronaut:

It all began with a telephone call from the White House to the Department of Defense. There was no arrogance in the callers voice; only a simple question:

"Does the Air Force have any Negroes in the new aerospace research pilots' course being set up at Edwards Air
Force Baser in California?"

After what was probably an extended pause came the answer: "No, there aren't any."

It was an ordinary enough question, but the call came
from an extraordinary source.

Had it come from an ordinary White House, the reaction
might have been mild, nothing more than grist for a work-
day tale some government employee could tell at a weekend
gathering. But this call came from the *Kennedy* White
House, that place called "Camelot," which had seen the beginning of civil rights "sit-ins" and had sent troops to get a
Black man into a university in the Deep South. It was a
White House that had used its influence to gain Martin Luther King's release from jail. Perhaps the recipient of the
call knew all of this and felt a bit like a person in a closed
garage slowly filling with carbon monoxide. In any event,
the reaction was predictable: something had better be
done—and rather quickly. The innocuous-sounding call thus
became something of an edict.

The air force swiftly launched a search for a Black pilot
with the right amount of flying time, the "right academic
background, and one would could [*sic*] meet all the other
stringent requirements." Fortunately, air force personnel of-
ficers didn't have to look too far, for it was about that time
that Capt. Ed Dwight's application reached them.[42]

When you go looking for something, you can usually find it:
even if it means passing over more qualified opportunities or
individuals.

The Kennedy Administration found their magic flying Negro: the only problem was Dwight couldn't pass the requirements to be an astronaut. From Phelps' book, we learn Colonel
Chuck Yeager was the one man who dared judge Ed Dwight by
the content of his character instead of giving him an

---

[42] Phelps, *They Had a Dream*, 6.

immediate, Kennedy-Administration-approved pass because of the advantageous color of his skin:

> Meanwhile, Colonel Yeager's dim view of Dwight's abilities grew. Yeager later maintained that Dwight's abilities were so lacking "we set up a special tutoring program to get him through the academics, as I recall, he lacked the engineering [background] that the other students had."
> Yeager further observes that Dwight worked hard, as did his tutors, but adds that "Dwight just couldn't hack it . . . didn't keep up in flying." Yeager claims to have worked with Dwight on his flying, but he noted that "our students were flying at levels really beyond his experience. The only prejudice against Dwight," Yeager recalls, wagging a literary finger, "was the conviction that he was not qualified to be in the school" in the first place.[43]

For his part in not placing Dwight high enough in the training program, Yeager was called before multiple Civil Rights inquiries, who hounded him with a tenacity not seen until Eric "My People" Holder's Department of Justice got a hold of George Zimmerman.

This isn't a joke.

This happened.

Yes, the Black-Run America (BRA) virus had already infiltrated NASA at its earliest stages. Had Kennedy not been assassinated, who knows how many more Blacks would have been pushed into NASA?

The Astronaut

Waiting his turn at the helm of a flight simulator at a Boeing plant in Seattle, Ed Dwight, 30, sips his coffee in silence and listens as a dozen of his fellow astronaut-trainees banter among themselves. The first black accepted in the space program, Dwight feels like a pariah. Sure, some of the

---

[43] Ibid., 20.

guys sidle up to him occasionally. He assumes they figure it might be to their advantage to stay on good terms with him, since President Kennedy has taken a personal interest in his career. But others, Dwight believes, have decided to give him the cold shoulder. Despite having logged more than 2,000 hours as an Air Force test pilot, Dwight himself some-times jokes that President Kennedy "picked me out of a tur-nip patch" to become an astronaut. But he will never forget how deeply honored he felt in November 1961, when he re-ceived a personal letter from Kennedy asking him to apply for the space program. Come what may, he plans to prove himself worthy of his Commander in Chief's high regard.

Three days after the assassination Ed Dwight was uncer-emoniously dropped from the astronaut-training program. "When my protector was killed, I was out," he says.[44]

Ebony magazine would go deeper into just what the Kennedy Administration had in mind with their token, hand-selected Black astronaut candidate:

Dwight believes Kennedy's death had everything to do with his doom as an astronaut candidate. "It was 100 percent the death of Kennedy," he says. "Prior to Kennedy's death I was living awfully high on the hog. I had a private secretary. I was sending out 5,000 press photographs a month, and I made 176 speeches the first year I was in [the astronaut training program at Edwards Air Force Base, Calif.]." The Kennedy Administration tried to break away from the White-Protestant-male mold for its astronauts in the 1961 by including one black.[45]

Yes, John F. Kennedy and his negrophilic administration was promoting the Blackness of Dwight to the tune of an unflatter-ing chorus of silly propaganda.

---

[44] Plummer, et al., "Where We Were."
[45] Bennett, "The Sculptor Who Would Have."

In his autobiography, Dwight writes of his racially conscious selection by the Kennedy Administration as a noble crusade to "make a Negro astronaut":

> The question was how to generate interest in such an ambitious approach to educating a race of people that so thirsted for progress. We needed parents, teachers, and the youth themselves involved. How would one get the Negro community on board? Whitney Young's solution was simple. "Make a Negro astronaut!"

Space was the new frontier and President Eisenhower had created seven new American heroes, the "First Seven Astronauts." By creating a live, flesh and blood Negro astronaut and parade him around the country it would be more than symbolic. The personification of this astronaut would not only serve as a role model to all Negro youth, but also would raise consciousness, and plant seeds into the white American psyche. Namely that, if a Negro could fly into space meeting all the educational and physical challenges, how could a race of people that produced such an astronaut be denied equal rights, a thoroughly brilliant idea on the part of the keen visionary, Whitney M. Young Jr. [. . .]

The White House had a plan and it had worked. Kennedy wanted a Negro astronaut and he needed his decision and ultimate success to be highly publicized. Even though the entire idea was Whitney Young's brainchild, the President was the direct beneficiary. His stock in the community skyrocketed and he was immediately viewed as a "friend" to Negro people. He wanted every Negro parent and child in the United States to know that a Negro astronaut actually existed and the idea would give hope that young people would be inspired to get involved in science at an early age which is exactly what it takes to accede to the excellence required to perform in the "frontiers of space." [. . .]

The press onslaught within days after the announcement caught Yeager, and the Aerospace Research Pilot School staff, of guard. His question, "Why does the country need a "Nigra" in space?" was answered in spades (no pun intended). The press had gone crazy, but so had the citizenry of the United States and the rest of the world. Within days I had received more than one thousand speaking requests and this continued unabated at a rate of five hundred requests a week throughout my entire training period, compounded by the hundreds of fan letters and then awards. I had done nothing except being announced as the "First Negro Astronaut," but hundreds of offers for awards from every sector of American society both Negro and white rolled in. Over time I would the "Key" *[sic]* to nearly every major city in America as well as a few minor ones.[46]

All of this, without ever actually being an astronaut: just the Kennedy Administration's appointed (anointed?) Black avatar, forced upon NASA to solidify the Black vote.

It wasn't about space exploration for John F. Kennedy, it was about enriching Black people's self-esteem *at the expense of space exploration*: that's what Ed Dwight's affirmative action selection/mandate upon NASA represented.

Perhaps Tom Wolfe, writing in *The Right Stuff*, nails it best:

What finally got to Yeager, however, was the Ed Dwight case.

It had been early this year that Yeager got word from the brass that the President, John F. Kennedy, was determined that NASA have at least one Negro astronaut in their lineup. The whole process was to take place organically, however, as if in the natural order of things. Kennedy was leaning on the Defense Department, Defense was leaning on the Air Force brass, and they tossed the potato to Yeager. The pilot who had been singled out was an Air Force captain named Ed Dwight. He was to go through ARPS and be selected by NASA. The clouds developed soon enough. Dwight was enrolled in the basic flight test course along with twenty-five other candidates.

---

[46] Dwight, *Soaring on the Wings*, 203, 249, 253.

Only the top eleven students could enter ARPS's six-month space-flight course, which had limited facilities, and Dwight did not rank among the top eleven. Yeager didn't see how he could jump him over other young tigers, all of them desperate to become astronauts. Every week, it seemed like, a detachment of Civil Rights Division lawyers would turn up from Washington, from the Justice Department, which was headed by the President's brother Bobby. The lawyers squinted in the desert sunlight and asked a great many questions about the progress and treatment of Ed Dwight and took notes. Yeager kept saying he didn't see how he could simply jump Dwight over these other men. And the lawyers would come back the next week and squint some more and take some more notes.

There were days when ARPS seemed like the Ed Dwight case with a few classrooms and some military hardware appended. A compromise was finally struck in which Dwight would be admitted to the space-flight course, but only if every man who ranked above him was also admitted. That was how it came to pass that the next class had fourteen students instead of eleven and included Captain Dwight. Meantime, the White House, apparently, was signaling to the Negro press that Dwight was going to be "the first Negro astronaut," and he was being invited to make public appearances. He was being set up for a fall, because the chances of NASA accepting him as an astronaut appeared remote in any event.

The whole thing was baffling. On the upper reaches of the great ziggurat the subject of race had never been introduced before. The unspoken premise was that you either had the right stuff or you didn't, and no other variables mattered. When the seven Mercury astronauts had been chosen in 1959, the fact that they were all white and all Protestant seemed to be interpreted as wholly benign evidence of their Small-Town American virtues. But by now, four years later, Kennedy, who had been supported by a coalition of minority groups in the 1960 election, had begun to raise the question of race as a matter of public policy in many areas. The phrase "white Protestant" took on a different meaning, so that it was now possible to regard the astronauts as some sort of cadre of whites of northern European racial back-ground. In fact, this had nothing to do, per se, with their being astronauts. It was typical of career military officers generally. Throughout the world, for that matter, career of-ficers came from "native" or "old settler" stock. Even in Is-rael, which had existed for barely a generation as an inde-pendent nation and was dominated politically by immi-grants from Eastern Europe, the officer corps was made up overwhelmingly of "real Israelis"—men born or raised from an early age in the pre-war Jewish settlements of the old Palestine. The other common denominator of the astronauts was that they were all first or only sons; yet not even this had any special significance, for studies soon showed that first or only sons dominated many occupations, including scholarly ones.

(In an age when the average number of children per fam-ily was barely more than two, the odds were two out of three that any male would be a first or only son). None of which was going to mollify the White House, however, because the astronaut, the single-combat warrior, had become a crea-ture with greater political significance than any other type of pilot in history.[47]

Had John F. Kennedy not been assassinated, there is no doubt Ed Dwight would have been forced on the Apollo missions to the Moon, and been the exalted first non-White to walk to on Earth's satellite. In this alternate history of America, it's highly likely he'd have been the first Black man elected presi-dent.

From its very inception, NASA was infected with the BRA virus.

---

[47] Wolfe, *Right Stuff*, 338–40.

But thanks to a test pilot who stood his ground, Ed Dwight never got the chance to be pushed into being an astronaut; instead, he was just used by the Kennedy Administration as the token Black candidate, to parade before the media to showcase their anti-racist attitude.

Once Lee Harvey Oswald fired his rifle in Dallas, Texas on that November 1963 day, Ed Dwight's role as the magical space Negro ended.

14

[Chuck] Yeager Bombed

May 10th, 2014

Ed Dwight.

Captain Ed Dwight.

In some alternate version of history, Dwight was the first Black man to walk on the Moon.

But that's not the case in our reality.

Thanks to Chuck Yeager.

In *Yeager: An Autobiography* by General Chuck Yeager and Leo Janos, we get an inside glimpse at one of the most amazing moments in American history.

The time a lone White man dared tell the entire establishment, pushing their Black avatar, "no."

The year is 1962.

The first class of pilots selected to undergo astronaut training—this after the astronauts had been selected for the Mercury team—was assembled and prepared to train at Edwards Air Force Base. Only problem? It was all White:

From the moment we picked our first class, I was caught in a buzz saw of controversy involving a black student. The White House, Congress, and civil rights groups came at me with meat cleavers, and the only way I could save my head was to prove I was a damned bigot.

In late 1961, we were ready to start screening applications for our first class at the space school, and because they would be the first bunch, the screening process was particu-larly thorough. We wanted only the very best pilots, and our first couple of classes consisted of experienced military test pilots, who had graduated from Edward's test pilot school, and whose abilities and academic background were demon-strably outstanding. Our space course was six months of in-tensive classroom work and flight training. My staff at Ed-wards culled the applications, pulled out the most promising student candidates, conducted preliminary checks of their records, and forwarded their recommendations to a selec-tion committee at the Pentagon, which carefully reviewed the background of each applicant, conducted personal inter-views, sought evaluations from their superiors, and further winnowed the list.

I was a member of the final selection committee, and af-ter several months of interviewing and tough deciding, we published our list of the first eleven students. Actually, we had 26 names in order of preference, but we didn't publish our list that way: we just named 11 guys alphabetically as the members of our first class, and listed the first three or four alternates, in case any of them dropped out.

The quality of those selected was such that they added tremendously to the prestige of our new school, which was our intention all along. I was thrilled with the choices. But when our list was published I received a phone call from the Chief of Staff's office asking whether any of the first 11 were black pilots. I said, no. Only one black pilot had applied for the course and he was number 26 on the list. I was informed that the White House wanted a black pilot in the space course.

The Chief of Staff was Gen. Curtis LeMay, probably the most controversial personality in the Air Force, since his days as the tough, cigar-chewing head of SAC. I knew him pretty well. General LeMay wasn't what I would call a smoothie. He was blunt: you didn't have to read between the lines dealing with him.

He got on the phone and said, "Bobby Kennedy wants a colored in space. Get one into your course." I said, "Well,

General, it's gonna be difficult. We have one applicant, a captain named Dwight, who came out number 26. We already published our list with the 15 who made it, and it's going to be embarrassing to republish the list with Dwight's name on it because now everyone knows who the first 15 are." He said: "Okay, I'll just tell them they're too late for this first class." But a 150-millimeter shell came ripping in from the White House, and LeMay was told: "By God, you will have a black pilot in that program – *now!*" He called me back: "Do what you have to do, Yeager, but get that colored guy in." I said, "Okay, general, but what I think we ought to do is take at least 15 students in the first class, instead of 11, and make him number 15. Give me a little more money and I can handle this many in the school."

He agreed, and we brought Dwight in. Ed Dwight was an average pilot with an average academic background. He wasn't a bad pilot, but he wasn't exceptionally talented, either. Flying with a good bunch in a squadron, he would probably get by. But he just couldn't compete in the space course against the best of the crop of experienced military test pilots. In those days, there were still comparatively few black pilots in the Air Force, but Dwight sure as hell didn't represent the top of the talent pool. I had flown with outstanding pilots like Emmett Hatch and Eddie Lavelle; but unfortunately, guys of their quality didn't apply for the course. Dwight did. So we brought him in, set up a special tutoring program to get him through the academics because, as I recall, he lacked the engineering academics that all the other students had.

Hell, I felt for Dwight, remembering my own academic problems in test pilot's school. It's really a rough situation, and he didn't have a Jack Ridley working with him – a genius in explaining the most complicated problems in understandable language. He worked hard, and so did his tutors, but he just couldn't hack it. And he didn't keep up in flying. I worked with him on that, and so did other instructors; but our students were flying at levels of proficiency that were really beyond his experience. The only prejudice against

Dwight was a conviction shared by all the instructors that he was not qualified to be in the school.

So we had a problem. General LeMay had asked me to keep him informed about Dwight's progress and knew what was happening at Edwards. About halfway through the course, I flew to Washington to attend an Air Force banquet and was seated next to General LeMay. He asked me if there was any improvement with Dwight. I said, "No sir. We're having a lot of trouble just trying to keep him from getting so far behind the others that it will be hopeless. He's just not hacking it." The general grunted. The he looked me in the eye and said, "Chuck, if you want to wash out Dwight, I'll back you all the way." I about fell out of my chair.

But it didn't come to that. Dwight hung on and squeezed through. He got his diploma qualifying him to be the nation's first black astronaut, but NASA did not select him and a few powerful supporters in Washington demanded to know why. The finger of blame was pointed at the school and I was hauled on the carpet to answer charges of racism raised by Dwight and some of his friends.

All hell broke loose. A few black congressmen announced they would launch an investigation of the incident, and the Air Force counselor, their chief lawyer, flew to Edwards from the Pentagon to personally take charge of the case. Man, I was hot. I told that lawyer, "You do not have a case of discrimination here. The White House discriminated by forcing us to take an unqualified guy. And we would have discriminated by passing him because he was black." Maybe "discrimination" was the wrong word, but I made my point. Anyway, the decision was made to fly in a group of black civil rights attorneys and a few congressmen and show them Dwight's school records.

I met with them. I said, "I'm the commandant of this school, but the truth is that I lack the college education to qualify as a NASA astronaut. It so happens, I couldn't care less. But if I did care a lot, there isn't a damned thing I could do about it because the regulations say I must have a college degree. Captain Dwight may care a lot about getting a diploma from this school, but the fact is he lacks the academic background and the flying skill to do it. Anyone with his grades deserved to be washed out, or it would be discrimination in reverse. Now, here are his complete school records from day one. Let's review them page by page."

The group had no idea that he had received special tutoring and was shocked to see his poor grades; they were satisfied that prejudice was in no way involved in this case. But that wasn't quite the end of it. I was so damned mad that I told the Air Force lawyer, "Hey, I want to file some charges of my own. I'm a full colonel and he's a captain, and I want to charge with insubordination. If he brought charges against me and couldn't make them stick, I want that guy court-martialed." I was told, no way; the Air Force would not allow that to happen because they taken enough heat over this matter already.

I was disgusted. I knew damned well that Dwight had taken a cheap shot at my West Virginia accent to try to save face. Hell, if I had been from Philadelphia or New York, he wouldn't have even tried. He was prejudiced against me, figuring that anyone from my part of the world was a redneck bigot. Many Southern whites who are honest will admit having problems about race in a general sense, but I didn't have to be the type who thought of all blacks as niggers to flunk Ed Dwight. And what really hurt was that the guy called into question not only my professional integrity, but also my most basic loyalty to the Air Force, which had allowed me to climb as high as my talents would take me. Ignoring the fact that I was a raw kid, often made fun of as a hillbilly, they gave me a chance to crawl in the cockpit of an expensive airplane and prove that I had what it took to fly that thing. I knew prejudice. I ran up against officers who looked down their noses at my ways and accent and pegged me as a dumb, down-home squirrel-shooter. But, damn it, the Air Force as an institution never let me down for an instant. In spite of where I came from or what I lacked, they trained me and gave me every opportunity to prove myself.

Nowadays, it has become fashionable for some companies to advertise themselves as "equal opportunity employers." The Air Force practiced that with me right from the start, and I would never deny to anybody else the chance to prove his worth, no matter who or what he is. There never were black pilots or white pilots in the Air Force. There were only pilots who knew how to fly, and pilots who didn't.[48]

There still aren't that many Black pilots in the United States Air Force or United States Navy.[49]

Knowing that Capt. Ed Dwight came in twenty-sixth out of twenty-six applicants (before his Blackness helped him get into the astronaut training program), should punctuate why the story of the Tuskegee Airmen is truly a celebration of segregation.[50]

Had those Black pilots who trained in Tuskegee, Alabama been forced to compete with White fighter pilots, well, they'd likely have come in last just as Capt. Dwight did.

The history of America post-World War II is nothing more than a never-ending quest to uplift Black people by any means possible.

In the process, wherever Black people have been uplifted, that portion of society—be it in government, academia, entertainment, sports, a neighborhood or community—has regressed to the Black mean.

It's fitting that one man, Chuck Yeager, broke the back of those pushing for the first Black astronaut.

Not only did he break the sound barrier, but he broke the power of those pushing Black-Run America (BRA) by simply saying "no."

Talk about *the right stuff.*

---

[48] Yeager and Janos, *Yeager*, 342–7.
[49] Burgess, "Despite recruitment efforts."
[50] See Kersey, "Segregation."

15

The Last Gasp of the Harvard Establishment: Obama Gives Hundreds of Millions to Failed HBCUs and Works to Protect Blacks from Repaying Student Loans

May 15th, 2014

He who laughs last, laughs best.

It was back in September 2012 when President Obama awarded $226 million to perpetually failing, underperforming, anemic, woeful (insert your desired synonym for "sucking") Historical Black Colleges and Universities.

You know, those centers of world-class education providers known as HBCUs.[51]

It was only a few years ago that NASA gave one of the HBCUs' worst-performing institutions, Morgan State, a $28.5 million grant (out of a five-year plan to give $95.8 million).[52]

Yes, the NASA Goddard Space Flight Center gave more than a quarter-hundred-million dollars to a school where admission requirements demand first-time freshmen have had a high school GPA of at least 2.0, an 850 SAT (combined critical reading and math), or a seventeen on their ACT.

Now the good people at Judicial Watch have uncovered the Obama Administration's stalwart policy of judging people (and institutions) entirely by the color of their skin.

Content of character?

---

[51] Wright, "Obama White House Awards HBCUs."
[52] Black Voice News, "HBCU Morgan State University."

If we judged HBCU's by the "content of character" displayed by their board of trustees and administrators, every one of them would shut down immediately, and every degree they awarded would be voided.

What was it that Judicial Watch uncovered?

The federal government violates its own student loan rules and wastes hundreds of millions of dollars to subsidize perpetually failing black colleges, including the alma mater of pop star Michael Jackson's criminally-convicted doctor, a Judicial Watch investigation has found.

The institutions are known as Historically Black Colleges and Universities (HBCU) and JW's probe has uncovered documents that show American taxpayers are being forced to fund them even when their accreditation has been stripped, they have dismal graduation rates and rank among the nation's worst medical schools. For instance, Meharry Medical College (where the late Jackson's physician, Conrad Murray, got his degree) is renowned for producing an alarming number of inept doctors along with third-world institutions like Manila Central University in the Philippines and the Autonomous University of Guadalajara in Mexico, according to records obtained by JW.

Yet the government continues giving it—and other troubled black colleges—large sums of money in the form of low-interest "loans" that are usually defaulted. This is done through the Historically Black College and University Capital Financing Program and it's proven to be a massive boondoggle. Obtained from a variety of government sources—including the U.S. Treasury and the Department of Education—the files accessed by JW show that the scandalous investment is not only fleecing taxpayers, it's also breaking rules created by the Obama administration under a 2010 measure that replaced student loans by private lenders with direct loans by the U.S. government.

Once its own money was in the game, the government decided that student loan lending rules were too loose and default rates were too high. In October 2011, the

Department of Education quietly changed underwriting criteria for the transactions, known as PLUS student
loans. Those criteria are still pretty low ("prospective borrowers can't have any current accounts more than 90 days
delinquent, or any foreclosures, bankruptcies, tax liens,
wage garnishments or defaults within the past five years.
But the department doesn't look at prospective borrowers'
incomes or their current debt load, meaning that poor borrowers with little or no credit history can be approved"), but
still resulted in a 10% increase in the denial rate.

Historically black colleges and universities were most adversely impacted by the new credit standards and HBCU officials as well as African American community leaders lob-
bied the Education Department to change the standards.
Education Secretary Arne Duncan apologized about the un-
intended effect on black colleges but publicly maintained
that "our department is required to carry out the law as it
was designed to protect parents and taxpayers against un-
affordable loans." Duncan did admit that that the process
could have been handled better and that internal and exter-
nal communications were "poor," according to a mainstream
newspaper.

Behind the scenes his agency quickly circumvented those
"laws to protect parents and taxpayers." In fact, Duncan
sent a letter to the Congressional Black Caucus regarding
the impact that the new loan rules were having on HBCUs
stating that the Department had "used [its] authority to consider 'extenuating circumstances' as a method to provide immediate relief for many students, which allowed previous
PLUS loan recipients and applicants whose adverse credit
determinations were based on a 'de minimis' amount of debt
to obtain a loan through the reconsideration process."

The agency has used the accommodation to provide near-
blanket approvals for PLUS loan applications from previous
recipients, according to the records obtained by JW. This academic year, about a third of the applicants from historically
black colleges denied this year were eligible to appeal. Of
those, 38 percent, or just over 8,000 applicants, filed for

reconsideration. Virtually all of them—98.5 percent—were then approved for a PLUS loan, the records show.

So why does the government continue pouring enormous sums of money into these failing institutions that often can't even keep their accreditation? The only explanation JW could find among the droves of government records is the Obama administration's determination of "the im-portance of HBCUs as a national resource."[53]

The way things are going, all non-Whites will soon be forgiven in repaying their student loan debt, with the 401(k) and retire-ment savings of White baby boomers and White retirees confis-cated to amend this grievous inequity.

What does this return on investment get the US taxpayer, besides an ever-expanding racial achievement gap, and Black college graduates with a piece of paper full of sound and fury, signifying nothing?

The findings on graduation rates at HBCUs published in the *Journal of Blacks in Higher Education* does the talking for us:

> The highest Black student graduation rate at the HBCUs is at Spelman College in Atlanta. There, 79 percent of entering students graduate from Spelman within six years. This rate is higher than the Black student graduation rate at many of the nation's highest-ranked colleges and universities. The Black student graduation at Spelman College is 15 percent-age points higher than at any other HBCU in our survey.
>
> The Black student graduation rate at Howard University is 64 percent. This ranks Howard second among the HBCUs in our survey. Morehouse College in Atlanta ranks third with a Black student graduation rate of 61 percent.
>
> The only other HBCU in our survey with a Black student graduation rate of more than 50 percent is Hampton

---

[53] Judicial Watch, "U.S. Pours Millions."

University in Virginia. There, 54 percent of entering Black students earn a degree at Hampton within six years.

At nearly half the HBCUs in our survey, the Black student graduation rate is 33 percent or lower. At these institutions, less than one third of all entering African American students earned a bachelor's degree within six years. There are six HBCUs in our survey where less than one in five entering Black students earn a bachelor's degree within six years.[54]

There is a new color bar in America. It favors every shade of black or brown, with those beating the Paper Bag Test allowed to advance to the front of line and have a leadership role in what we've dubbed Black-Run America.

We could have been on Mars, but we had to pour billions of dollars into HBCUs.

The space program produced numerous spin-off technologies and gave us hope for the future of nation.

Investing billions in HBCUs has only produced more empirical evidence on the reality of racial differences, providing more and more reasons to validate the realization our nation has no future.

Save that of Detroit.

---

[54] Journal of Blacks in Higher Education, "Tracking Graduation Rates."

16

Norman Mailer Long Ago, Heard It on the Sea of Tranquility:
Remembering *Of a Fire on the Moon*

May 31st, 2014

For the moment, we find ourselves on the losing side of history.

This situation will change, but for now, we are losing.

It's during the 45th anniversary year of the landing on the Moon (the July 20th 1969 lunar mission should have ushered in a new era for mankind; instead we've been actively pursuing policies to take us back to the stone age, by transferring wealth from Whites to pay for fecund Blacks and brown people) that we should pause, and reflect on what this moment truly represented.

Norman Mailer did.

The longtime leftist agitator wrote a book on NASA's mission to put a man on the Moon by the end of 1960s, and it contains one of the more profound observations you'll ever find describing what Neil Armstrong's journey represented.

An almost forgotten book, *Of a Fire on the Moon*, Mailer expends a lot of energy deriding White Anglo-Saxon Protestant (WASP) America's ambitions to travel to the stars, and the apprehension he felt toward a new era dawning for Mankind.

This era never came; instead, we entered an era when an 83 percent Black city could declare the largest bankruptcy in US history. No one would dare notice it was because of the collective efforts of individual Black people that Detroit was now the

world's greatest experiment, proving racial differences in intelligence and behavior exist.

Consequently, just as NASA notes—bemoans—in the chapter called "Social, Cultural, and Educational Legacies: NASA
Reflects America's Changing Opportunities; NASA Impacts US
Culture" in *Wings in Orbit*, it was the collective effort of individual White people who put a man on the Moon.[55]

Discrimination and a belief in merit gave us the July 20th,
1969 Moon landing; a steadfast belief in legislation against discrimination and removing any qualification with quota-based
government hiring gave us 2014 Detroit.

But let's get back to Mailer's book *Of a Fire on the Moon*.
Going by the alias "Aquarius," Mailer writes of a party he at-
tended in Houston while the three White astronauts were com-
pleting the journey to the Moon.

At the party, he encountered a usually loquacious black Ivy
League professor (who espoused some form of 'Black Power'
and mentored Black students on campus), who was uncharac-
teristically laconic and drinking heavily. Mailer writes:

> He was normally so elegant a man that it was impossible to
> conceive of how he would make a crude move—now, you
> could know. Something raucous and jeering was still with-
> held, but the sourness of his stomach had gotten into the
> sourness of his face. His collar was a hint wilted.[56]

It is here Mailer unloads with the most masterful part of his
book, observing the source of the Black Ivy League professor's
angst:

> But there were other reasons for drinking as well. America
> had put two White men on the moon, and lifted them off. A
> triumph of White men was being celebrated in the streets of

---

[55] Ross-Nazzal and Lucis, "NASA Reflects," in NASA, *Wings in Orbit*.
[56] Mailer, *Of a Fire on the Moon*, 124.

this city. It was even worse than that. For the developed abilities of these White men, their production, their flight skills, their engineering feats, were the most successful part of that White superstructure which had been strangling the possibilities of his own Black people for years. The professor was an academic with no mean knowledge of colonial strug- gles of colored peoples. He was also a militant. If the degree of his militancy was not precisely defined, still its presence was not denied.

His skin was dark. If he were to say, "Black is beautiful" with a cultivated smile, nonetheless he was still saying it. Aquarius had never been invited to enter this Black man's vision, but it was no great mystery the Black believed his people were possessed of a potential genius which was greater than Whites. Kept in incubation for two millennia, they would be all the more powerful when they prevailed. It was nothing less than a great civilization they were pre- pared to create. Aquarius could not picture the details of that civilization in the Black professor's mind, but they had talked enough to know they agreed that this potential great- ness of the Black people was not to be found in technology.

Whites might need the radio to become tribal but Blacks would have another communion. From the depth of one con- sciousness they could be ready to speak to the depth of an- other; by telepathy might they send their word. That was the logic implicit in CPT. If CPT was one of the jokes by which Blacks admitted Whites to the threshold of their view, it was a relief to learn that CPT stood for Colored People's Time. When a black friend said he would arrive at 8 p.m. and came after midnight, there was still logic in his move. He was traveling on CPT. The vibrations he received at 8 p.m. were not sufficiently interesting to make him travel to- ward you—all that was hurt were the host's undue expecta- tions. The real logic of CPT was that when there was trouble or happiness the brothers would come on the wave.

Well, white technology was not built on telepathy, it was built on electromagnetic circuits of transmission and recep- tion, it was built on factory workers pressing their button or

monitoring their function according to firm and bound stations of the clock. The time of a rocket mission was Ground
Elapsed Time, GET. Every sequence of the flight was tied
into the pure numbers of the time line.

So the flight to the moon was a victory for GET, and the
first heats of the triumph suggested that the fundamental
notion of Black superiority might be incorrect: in this hour,
it would no longer be as easy for a militant Black to say that
Whitey had built a palace on numbers, and numbers killed
a man, and numbers would kill Whitey's civilization before
all this was through. Yesterday, Whitey with his numbers
had taken a first step to the stars, taken it ahead of Black
men. How that had to burn in the ducts of this Black man's
stomach, in the vats of his liver.

Aquarius thought again of the lunar air of technologists.
Like the moon, they traveled without a personal atmosphere. No wonder Blacks had distaste for numbers, and
found trouble studying. It was not because they came—as
liberals necessarily would have it—from wrecked homes and
slum conditions, from drug-pushing streets, no, that kind of
violence and disruption could be the pain of a people so rich
in awareness they could not bear the deadening jolts of a
civilization on each of their senses. Blacks had distaste for
numbers not because they were stupid or deprived, but because numbers were abstracted from the sense, numbers
made you ignore the taste of the apples for the amount in
the box, and so the use of numbers shrunk the protective
envelope of human atmosphere, eroded that extrasensory
aura which gave awareness, grace, the ability to move one's
body and excel at sports and dance and war, or be able to
travel on an inner space of sound. Blacks were not the only
ones who hated numbers—how many attractive women
could not bear to add a column or calculate a cost. Numbers
were a pestilence to beauty.

There was something to be said after all for arriving on
time. CPT was excellent for the nervous system if you were
the one to amble in at midnight, but Aquarius had played
the host too often.

"You know," said the professor, "there are no Black as-tronauts."

"Of course not."

"Look," said the Black professor, "do they have any awareness of how the money they spent could have been used?"

"They have a very good argument: they say if you stopped space tomorrow, only a token of the funds would go to pov-erty."

"I'd like to be in a position to argue about that," said the Black. "Damn," he said, "are they still on the moon?"

"They took off already," said Aquarius.

"No trouble?"

"None."

If the Blacks yet built a civilization, magic would be at its heart. For they lived with the wonders of magic as the Whites lived with technology. How many Blacks had made a move or inhibited it because the emanations of the full moon might affect their cause. Now Whitey had walked the moon, put his feet on it. The moon presumably had not spo-ken. Or had it, and Richard Nixon received the favor and Teddy Kennedy the curse? Was there no magic to combat technology? Then the strength of Black culture was stricken. There would not be a future Black civilization, merely an adjunct to the White. What lava in the raw mem-branes of the belly. The Black professor had cause to drink. The moon shot had smashed more than one oncoming supe-riority of the Black.[57]

For the moment, we find ourselves on the losing side of history.

This situation will change, but for now, we are losing.

Our civilization has been on CPT (Colored People's Time) for too long.

Much.

Too.

Long.

---

[57] Ibid., 125–7.

As NASA's own publication makes clear, the agency was forced to go on CPT by the state in the early 1970s.[58]

But Mailer's words make clear what the successful Apollo 11 mission meant—may those of European ancestry remember them well.

For history will stop beating to the clock of CPT.

---

[58] NASA, *Wings in Orbit.*

17

"It's a Joke. It's All a Joke. Mother Forgive Me."

May 5th, 2014

Edward R. Murrow destroyed Joseph R. McCarthy's career, in a move later celebrated via a movie produced by George Clooney.

As head of the United States Information Agency (the USIA's mission was "to understand, inform and influence for-eign publics in promotion of the national interest, and to broaden the dialogue between Americans and US institutions, and their counterparts abroad") in the early 1960s, he sent a memo to James Webb.

Webb was then the administrator of NASA.

America was then a nation roughly 90 percent white and 10 percent black. Here's what the memo read:

September 21st, 1961

Dear Jim,

Why don't we put the first non-white man in space?

If your boys were to enroll and train a qualified Negro and then fly him in whatever vehicle is available, we could retell our whole space effort to the whole non-white world, which is most of it.

As ever,

Yours,

Edward R. Murrow[59]

---

[59] Memorandum by Edward R. Murrow, in Atkinson, *The Real Stuff.*

The only monuments non-Whites build to the memory of Whites are to men like John Brown (in the heart of Port-au-Prince, Haiti, rests Avenue John Brown).

Put this in the wing of the new African-American museum in Washington, D.C. Call the wing, "Black History That Should Have Been" (along with the picture of Capt. Edward Dwight putting the American flag on the Moon).

This memo was found in *Real Stuff: History of National Aeronautics and Space Administration's Astronaut Recruitment Program.*

If you aren't laughing yet, you'll never understand the joke.

18

"Tranquility Base Here. The Eagle Is Down":
In the End, Rev. Abernathy's Vision Wins Out

April 26th, 2013

Two seemingly unrelated stories (one a press release from
the US Treasury Department issued on April 23rd, 2013; the
other an excerpt from a book on NASA and Space Flight) illus-
trate the current state of America better than any speech by a
Conservatism Inc. politician, or oration by a Marxist ensconced
in academia.

No need for any analysis, for the narrative should leap from
your computer screen and knock you over the head with a fe-
rocity usually reserved for the boxing ring:

Washington, DC—Building on the Obama Administration's
commitment to increase economic opportunity in distressed
areas of the United States, the U.S. Department of the
Treasury's Community Development Financial Institutions
Fund (CDFI Fund) today announced $3.5 billion in New
Markets Tax Credit (NMTC) awards nationwide. Treasury
will provide 85 organizations with tax credit allocation authority under the tenth award round of the NMTC Program.

"The New Markets Tax Credit addresses one of the most
significant obstacles to economic development that low-income communities face: a lack of access to patient, private
investment capital," said Treasury Assistant Secretary for
Financial Institutions Cyrus Amir-Mokri. "The $31 billion

worth of tax credits awarded in past years have gone toward preserving hundreds of thousands of jobs and bringing community facilities and new businesses into neighborhoods that desperately needed them. I expect today's awardees will continue that trend."

"In fact, over 70 percent of New Markets Tax Credit investments have been made in communities that meet the highest distress criteria, above even the program's requirements, CDFI Fund Director Donna J. Gambrell. "That result effectively demonstrates how essential the New Markets Tax Credit Program is to spurring economic development in underserved areas."

The NMTC, established by Congress in December 2000, permits individual and corporate taxpayers to receive a credit against federal income taxes for making equity investments in vehicles known as Community Development Entities. The credit provided to the investor totals 39 percent of the cost of the investment and is claimed over a seven-year period. For every dollar invested by the Federal government, the NMTC Program generates over eight dollars in private investment. This strong record of spurring economic growth is one of the reasons why President Obama's FY14 budget included an expansion and permanent extension of the New Markets Tax Credit.

The 85 organizations receiving awards under the 2012 round were selected from a pool of 282 applicants that requested approximately $21.9 billion. . . .

Since its creation in 1994, the CDFI Fund has awarded over $1.7 billion to CDFIs, community development organizations, and financial institutions through the CDFI Program, the Bank Enterprise Awards Program, the Capital Magnet Fund, the Financial Education and Counseling Pilot Program, and the Native American CDFI Assistance Program. In addition, the CDFI Fund has allocated $36.5 billion in tax credit authority to Community Development Entities through the New Markets Tax Credit Program.[60]

---

[60] US Department of the Treasury. "Treasury Announces $3.5 Billion."

In T.A. Heppenheimer's book *The Space Shuttle Decision* we learn that as one branch of mankind of was preparing to send a man to the Moon, another branch of mankind was busy trying to see money invested in such a frivolous endeavor channeled to their community. From the chapter "Winter of Discontent":

On an afternoon in July 1969, while the Apollo 11 mission stood poised for a flight to the moon, Tom Paine found himself confronted by a group of civil rights demonstrators. Their leader was Reverend Ralph Abernathy, president of the Southern Christian Leadership Conference. Abernathy had succeeded Martin Luther King in that post, following the death of King a year earlier. Abernathy now came to Cape Canaveral on the eve of NASA's triumph. A light mist of rain fell intermittently, as thunder rumbled in the distance. Paine stood coatless under a cloudy sky, accompanied only by NASA's press officer, as Abernathy approached with his party, marching slowly and singing "We Shall Overcome." Several mules were in the lead, as symbols of rural poverty. Abernathy then gave a short speech.

He deplored the condition of the nation's poor, declaring that one-fifth of the nation lacked adequate food, clothing, shelter, and medical care. In the face of such suffering, he asserted that space flight represented an inhuman priority. He urged that its funds be spent to feed the hungry, clothe the naked, tend the sick, and house the homeless.

Paine replied that "if we could solve the problems of poverty by not pushing the button to launch men to the moon tomorrow, then we would not push that button." He added that NASA's technical advances were "child's play" compared to "the tremendously difficult human problems" that concerned the SCLC. He offered the hope that NASA indeed might contribute to addressing these problems, and then asked Abernathy, a minister, to pray for the safety of the astronauts. Abernathy answered with emotion that he would certainly do this, and they ended this impromptu meeting by shaking hands all around.

Their brief conversation brought no lasting consequence. Yet it was heavy with history, for Paine and Abernathy stood as representatives of two deep themes that had marked the nation's experience before America even existed.

Paine was the technologist, heir to a record of splendid accomplishment. His forebears had built ships, constructed transcontinental railroads, dug the Panama Canal, captured water to allow cities to grow in the arid West, flung power and telephone lines from coast to coast. They had built highways and factories, had put the nation on wheels, had mastered the art of flight. At that very moment, others were winning achievement in the realm of computers.

There was, however, another and far more somber side to America's history, for the nation had been conceived in the original sin of slavery. Abraham Lincoln had proposed that "every drop of blood drawn with the lash shall be paid by another drawn with the sword"; yet the stain ran so deep that not even the Civil War could expunge it. Like Lincoln, Martin Luther King had grappled with this sin, had sought the moral authority to sway a deeply divided people; and like Lincoln, he had paid with his life, with his goal only partly won.[61]

One branch of mankind succeeded on walking on the Moon. Every time you look up at the Moon—be it a full, waxing, or waning Moon—know that the only feet to ever tread upon it are those of Europeans.

But know this—though the problems of poverty were not solved back in 1969 and we did send men to the Moon, Reverend Abernathy's dreams came true in the end.

Space flight and exploration isn't an "inhuman priority"—it's a priority of a civilization unencumbered by being tethered finite.

---

[61] Heppenheimer, *Space Shuttle Decision*, 151–2.

A belief in our supremacy got us to the Moon, propelled by the dreams of a better tomorrow for our posterity and our nation; a belief in our shared guilt gave us Detroit 2013, propelled by the nightmares our forefathers stained their progeny with.

Now, we give tax-credits in the billions to areas blighted by the same people who forty-four years ago stood against one branch of mankind's greatest technological achievement—whining for food, clothing, shelter, and medical care.

One small step for a man, one giant leap for mankind.

Few people know a speech was prepared for President Nixon in the event the Apollo mission experienced problems:

> Fate has ordained that the men who went to the Moon to explore in peace will stay on the moon to rest in peace. These brave men, Neil Armstrong and Edwin [Buzz] Aldrin, know that there is no hope for their recovery. But they also know that there is hope for mankind in their sacrifice.[62]

What hope is there for mankind in the sacrifice of Detroit? Of Birmingham? Of Memphis? Of Baltimore? Of St. Louis? Of Philadelphia? Of Milwaukee? Of Chicago?

Civilization has been sacrificed in these cities.

---

[62] William Safire to H. R. Haldeman, "In Event of Moon Disaster."

19

Does the Flag Still Stand for Freedom: Or Did "They" Take that Away?

June 16th, 2014

With apologies to Lee Greenwood, but does the flag still stand for freedom?

Or did "they" get around to taking that away?

And who's the "they" in the song Greenwood hawks to crowds still high on the patriotic chords only a man of Lloyd Marcus' talent could reach?

Sadly, the flag of a far different nation than the one we currently live in is—in all probability—dust in the solar wind (with apologies to Kansas).

I'm referring to the various flags the Apollo crews placed on the Moon:

Do the Apollo flags remain where they were planted or have they fallen or have they disintegrated after four decades of exposure the lunar environment? . . . A variety of recent media articles report current thinking on the condition of the flags. Here is a sampling:

Reichhardt, Tony, *Finding Apollo*, Air and Space, Smithsonian Institution, September 2008: "The (Apollo 11's) flag is probably gone. Buzz Aldrin saw it knocked over by the rocket blast as he and Neil Armstrong left the moon 39 summers ago. Lying there in the lunar dust, unprotected from the sun's harsh ultraviolet rays, the flag's red and blue would have bleached white in no time. Over the years, the nylon would have turned brittle and disintegrated. . . . Dennis Lacarrubba, whose New Jersey-based company, Annin, made the flag and sold it to NASA for $5.50 in 1969, considers what might happen to an ordinary nylon flag left outside for 39 years on Earth, let alone on the moon. He thinks for a few seconds. 'I can't believe there would be anything left,' he concludes. 'I gotta be honest with you. It's gonna be ashes.'"

Chow, Denise, *On the Moon, Flags & Footprints of Apollo Astronauts Won't Last Forever*, Space.com, September 2011: "Based on the new (LRO) images, that mystery may remain unsolved, but (LRO Camera Principal Investigator, Dr. Mark) Robinson is skeptical that the flags are intact, if they are still there. The moon's extreme heat and ultraviolet conditions would probably destroy the nylon flags over time, he explained. 'Personally, I would be surprised if there's anything left on them,' Robinson said. 'You know how [if] you leave a flag out over summer, how it starts to fade. Now, imagine the extreme UV environment on the moon, and the hot and cold cycling, and it's been 40 years—so if the flags are still there, they're probably in pretty rough shape. . . .' (Robert Pearlman, an expert on space history and collectibles, and editor of collectSPACE.com said) 'We didn't design a special American flag to go to the moon to last thousands of years. They literally sent out a secretary to the nearby Sears and bought an off-the-shelf flag and modified it. The natural disintegration of the flag's material in the harsh conditions on the moon's surface is to be expected.'"

Axelrod, Jim, *What happened to the American flags on the moon?*, CBS News, July 2011: "(Historian Anne Platoff) believes the first two (flags) from Apollo 11 and 12 did not survive the ignition gases of the lunar liftoff. . . . 'It wasn't the intention for the flag material itself to last. It was just to be there during the event—the landing and departing from the moon. We didn't have a requirement that the flag, the U.S. flag, had to withstand all the environments for eons.' Made from nylon just like the ones at a dime store, though ordered off the shelf from a government supply

catalogue, Annie Platoff's theory is they are probably dark-
ened and maybe more than a bit tattered. 'I would guess,
over time, 40 years, the combination of sun-rot and micro-
meteor impact is probably devastating. I mean it's not a
pretty picture to paint. The only way you're going to test
these theories is to go back to the Moon and look at the flag,'
Platoff says."

Finally, Lunar Scientist Paul Spudis, in a July 2011 blog
posting, writes: "For forty-odd years, the flags have been exposed to the full fury of the Moon's environment—alternat-
ing 14 days of searing sunlight and 100° C heat with 14 days
of numbing-cold -150° C darkness. But even more damaging
is the intense ultraviolet (UV) radiation from the pure unfiltered sunlight on the cloth (modal) from which the Apollo
flags were made. Even on Earth, the colors of a cloth flag
flown in bright sunlight for many years will eventually fade
and need to be replaced. So it is likely that these symbols of
American achievement have been rendered blank, bleached
white by the UV radiation of unfiltered sunlight on the lunar surface. Some of them may even have begun to physi-
cally disintegrate under the intense flux."

"Bleached," "disintegrated," "ashes," "rough shape," and
"tattered." Intuitively, experts mostly think it highly un-
likely the Apollo flags (See Platoff's article "Where No Flag
Has Gone Before: Political and Technical Aspects of Placing
a Flag on the Moon" for details), could have endured the 42
years of exposure to vacuum, about 500 temperature swings
from 242 F during the day to -280 F during the night, micro-
meteorites, radiation and ultraviolet light, some thinking
the flags have all but disintegrated under such an assault of
the environment.[63]

Our finest hour was on July 20th, 1969.

But it was foolish to believe the flag would survive the harsh
reality of space, just as it was foolish to believe once proud cities like Memphis, Birmingham, Detroit, Jackson (MS), and

---

[63] Fincannon, "Six Flags on the Moon."

Baltimore would survive the harsh reality a majority black population creates.

"Bleached," "disintegrated," "ashes," "rough shape," and *"tattered."*

Funny how these adjectives describe not only the flag of the United States of America on the Moon, but the flag of "our" country in cities like Memphis, Birmingham, Detroit, Jackson, Baltimore, Los Angeles, Houston, Dallas, and San Antonio.

But it wasn't the solar wind that "disintegrated" the US flag, as was done to the ones placed on the Moon; it was the absence of a White population that did the trick.

Cue up Lee Greenwood one more time.

For old times' sake.

But ask yourself this serious question: solar radiation is a good reason for the United States of America's flag disintegrating on the Moon, but that reason doesn't fly as to why civilization has disintegrated in places like Detroit and Memphis back on Earth.

20

When *The New York Times* Published an Article Noting: "Blacks and Apollo: Most Couldn't Have Cared Less"

June 1st, 2014

"Our people went to the Moon. In 1969. With the slide rule."
Three simple sentences forever denoting an inherent truth so obvious it shouldn't even be necessary to spell out precisely what it means.

Instead, let's just note what Thomas A. Johnson filed for *The New York Times* on July 27th, 1969.

Supremacy is such an unnecessary word when Whites have the privilege of knowing the greatest achievement in recorded history was only possible due to their ancestors: seemingly insignificant White individuals' lives culminated in the collective expression of the July 20th 1969 Moon landing.

And as Johnson noted in *The New York Times*, Blacks couldn't have cared less:

> Many black Americans found ways in recent days to ignore the Apollo 11 moon shot, an effort, they say, ignored them.
>
> An estimated 50,000 people flocked to last Sunday's Harlem Cultural (soul music) Festival at Mt. Morris park and the single mention of the LM touching down on the moon brought boos from the audience.
>
> At the Metropolis Bar on 23rd Street and Michigan Avenue in Chicago the black patrons watched baseball games on television when the LM landed. The same was true in many Harlem bars.

"We're earth-bound," said one Harlem bar patron. He used the stubby fingers on his laborer's hard hand to enumerate—with an unbridled anger—some other reason for his setting a "Mets over the moon" priority.

"There ain't no brothers in the program where they can get into some of that big money," he said. "The whole thing uses money that should be spent right here on earth and I don't like them saying 'all good Americans are happy about it'—I damn sure ain't happy about it."

On Commitments

He expressed a resentment common to many Negroes surveyed last week. But he did not touch on another frequently stated—and probably the most serious—trigger for the black anger at the space program.

"It proves that white America will do whatever it is committed to doing," said Miss Sylvia Drew, to synthesize that point of anger.

Miss Drew, who is an attorney for the NAACP Legal Defense and Educational Fund, added: "If America fails to end discrimination, hunger and malnutrition then we must conclude that America is not committed to ending discrimination, hunger and malnutrition. Walking on the moon proves that we do what we want to do as a nation."

Miss Victoria Mares, the director of a poverty program in Saginaw, Michigan, compared the United States to "a man who has a large family—they have no shoes, no clothing, no food and the rent is overdue. But when he gets paid he runs out and buys himself a set—another set—of electric trains. We are supporting our Government's hobby at the expense of its poor citizens."

The NAACP executive director, Roy Wilkins, called the moon shot "a cause of shame," and added, "there's something wrong with the Government's priority system." And in Mississippi, Charles Evers said: "The billions of dollars spent on this moon exploration program means that it will be even longer before America begins to keep her promises to the poor."

The differences between the black and white reactions to the moon walk point up the deep sense of alienation that much of black America feels for this affluent society that seems to many to place real equality for the black and the poor in a priority behind those of the war in Vietnam, the space program and efforts to curb inflation.

And more and more, the million spent in Vietnam and in space serve to convince more and more black Americans that heir country can, indeed, "do whatever it is committed to do."

Dr. Benjamin W. Watkins, the honorary "Mayor of Harlem," wrote in the Negro weekly, the Amsterdam News, that the money could have best been spent on the rehabilitation of the cities. And noting the lack of response from the black community, he said: "the world does not stop even if a trio of astronauts get off it."

He added: "Whether black people showed any interest in the landing on Sunday is irrelevant. We in Harlem are demanding that the trio of astronauts include in their itinerary Harlem, Watts or some other ghetto, rather than Moscow or England."

A black writer who lives on Long Island said that he did not watch the moon walk except for a moment when he turned off the set in his children's room. "They had gone to sleep," he said, "and I saw they were about to step out of the LM and onto the moon. I said a prayer for two human beings out in that great unknown, then I turned it off and went back to work on a proposal for a poverty program."

The last line in an editorial in the Amsterdam News stated simply: "Yesterday the moon. Tomorrow, maybe us."[64]

"Yesterday the Moon. Tomorrow, Detroit."

A more responsible reading of what took place after the successful Moon landing on July 20th, 1969.

There was never going to be a peace.

---

[64] Johnson, "Blacks and Apollo."

Only hatred and resentment.

While one side constructed barriers to protect the fragility of Whiteness, the other side demanded we put the future on hold so the remnants of a retrograde species of humanity could catch up.

While one side landed on the Moon, the other side demanded more, more, and more.

Instead of cutting a path to the stars, we momentarily forfeited the future by traveling down a road paved with good intentions.

Now we know where such a path leads: Detroit.

Miss Sylvia Drew, White America has been committed to uplifting the Negro.

And it has failed at this obviously dysgenic endeavor.

No matter what happens in the United States of America, the record clearly shows we dismantled our civilization for the betterment of Black people. And still, we failed in our mission.

Three sentences disable even the most committed egalitarian's pablum, washing away years of intellectual rot in the process:

"Our people went to the Moon. In 1969. With the slide rule."

Securing our future was always about rescuing our past. Once this is accomplished, the present is overwhelmed instantly.

21

Wernher von Braun's Dream for the Future vs. Martin Luther King's Dream

May 1st, 2014

The left would have you believe not only that evolution is real—and that all those knuckle-dragging Christians are holding back true progress—but also that this evolution stopped cold with the different racial groups of humanity.

Maintaining the orthodoxy of equality requires a child-like faith in this trade-off.

Every other animal, beast, fish, reptile, and microorganism was touched by evolution, save humans. For race is nothing more than a social construct.

Right?

Wrong.

Regardless of whether you believe in evolution, it believes in you.

A divine belief in a creator doesn't qualify you as a nut, as those steadfast adherents to the divinity of the theory of evolution would try and make the general public believe.

Nor does a belief in evolution make you an enemy of faith and a divine creator.

Since July 20th, 1969, the United States of America has sunk tremendous resources into uplifting the Black population of this country.

This has been our de facto mission.

It was easier to land on the Moon than undo the harsh truths of evolution.

For just as Detroit rose from the ground Amerindians called a hunting terrain for centuries, in less than 40 years of continuous Black political rule it has regressed back to nature.

No matter the trivial nature of a White person's existence, it was their seemingly insignificant contributions to the progress of civilization that made Detroit into the "Paris of the West."

Stability.

Family.

Community.

Remove the people who create these conditions, and they instantly vanish.

Instability.

Chaos.

Ruin.

In Michael Neufeld's biography of the great scientist Wernher Von Braun, we get to read about when one man's dream captivated a people to strive for greatness off this tiny, spinning rock (today, only one man's dream is allowed to be the roadmap for the future; a roadmap with, inevitably, "Detroit 2014" as its final destination).

Von Braun: Dreamer of Space, Engineer of War contains Von Braun's opinion of what the first steps on Earth's natural satellite meant in the grand scheme of human history.

At a press conference, Neufeld said:

But it was Norman Mailer in His Apollo 11 book, *Of a Fire on the Moon*, who penned the most unforgettable portrait of von Braun at the Cape. During the prelaunch press conference, the Marshall director stole the show from Mueller, Debus, and the others when he issued the most quotable line of the afternoon. "When asked how he evaluated the importance of the act of putting a man on the moon, Von Braun answered, "I think it is equal in importance to that moment in evolution when aquatic life came crawling up on land."[65]

As outlined in a 1965 *Playboy* interview, Martin Luther King believed the American government (White people, the taxpay-ers, naturally) should have embarked on a plan to spend roughly $50 billion to uplift Black people. It was the January issue, when Hugh Hefner's magazine published this exchange:

Haley: Along with the other civil rights leaders, you have often proposed a massive program of economic aid, financed by the Federal Government, to improve the lot of the na-tion's 20,000,000 million Negroes. Just one of the projects you've mentioned . . . is expected to cost $141,000,000 over the next ten years, and that includes only Harlem. A nation-wide program such as you propose would undoubtedly run into the billions.

King: About 50 billion, actually—which is less than one year of our present defense spending. It is my belief that with the expenditure of this amount over a ten-year period, a genuine and dramatic transformation could be achieved in the conditions of Negro life in America. I am positive, more-over, that the money spend would be more than amply jus-tified by the benefits that would accrue to the nation through a spectacular decline in school dropouts, family breakups, crime rates, illegitimacy, swollen relief rolls, riot-ing and other social evils. [66]

Though four years later white America would land on the Moon, the implementation of Project Negro Uplift would over-take any other national campaign as the highest priority and loftiest moral goal.

And not one penny spent to uplift Blacks—as MLK was pos-itive it would—has gone to lower Black dropout rates, Black family breakups, Black crime rates, Black illegitimacy, Black

[65] Neufeld, *Von Braun*, 431.
[66] Haley, "Alex Haley Interviews Martin Luther King, Jr."

reliance on relief/welfare, or staved off Black rioting (mob assaults on Whites) and other Black-in-origin social evils.

Those American cities that have been at or near the top of the list of per-capita misery statistics—most murders, nonfatal gun violence, most addicts, most high school dropouts, lowest test scores in both math and reading comprehension, most cases of H.I.V. and syphilis—are all majority Black.

In some cases, the White population in those places is below 10 percent.

When man set foot on the Moon back on July 20th, 1969, a new step forward in evolution—as Wernher Von Braun correctly surmised—should have started.

In America, the exact opposite happened.

We made it a national policy to return life in this country to a level just above the primordial ooze we long emerged from; we made it national policy for devolution and *Idiocracy* to pave the way for our future.

Once, beneath the stars, in the mind of Wernher Von Braun, the universe was ours; today, beneath those same stars, our cities regress to the Black mean of the inhabitants found there.

Forget the stars: Detroit in 2014 isn't even ours.

With all due to respect to Wernher Von Braun, the moment when we understand racism has nothing to do with the plight of Black America, and everything to do with those racial differences evolution slipped into our genetic code (thus, reverting our national policy and efforts away from fulfilling Martin Luther King's fantasy and back to Von Braun's dream)—well, that's the moment we can look back to the stars and smile.

Remembering the tangible reality of evolution and how it touched the various races of mankind via the ruins of Detroit, and smiling when we once again see—in person—its reality, via the American flag White men planted on the Moon, back on July 20th, 1969.

Christopher Nolan's *Interstellar* Teaser Trailer: It Will Only Speak to White People About What We Lost and We Must Regain

December 15th, 2013

Christopher Nolan might have done it.

On the day China landed a moon rover on the Moon, signaling the dawn of the Chinese Century, a teaser trailer for Nolan's new movie, *Interstellar*, was released.

We already know America gave up on space travel and exploration, and instead decided to challenge nature herself by making the Black man live up to the White man's standards: the war on poverty was, in itself, a war on the civilization White people had established, bled and fought for in America.

In the process, our cities reverted to the standards set by the Black man.

Well, here's what Disingenuous White Liberals (DWL) believe *Interstellar* is about.

So, is Christopher Nolan's "Interstellar" gearing up to be the biggest blockbuster about agriculture ever? That's certainly the last word on it, as the always-secrecy-prone filmmaker hasn't let any details slip out about his new movie. Reports during the summer claimed that the future-set story "details the toll climate change has taken on agriculture, with corn the last crop to be cultivated. The scientists embark on a journey through a worm hole into other dimensions in search of somewhere other crops can be grown." This first trailer for the film certainly goes to the farm.

As per usual with Nolan, there's not much in the way of major reveals in this teaser (a good chunk of which is stock footage), but the shots of corn and farmland through history certainly suggest those early plot details aren't far off. Instead, the focus here is on the words delivered by Matthew McConaughey, which are as follows:

"We've always defined ourselves by the ability to overcome the impossible. And we count these moments, these moments when we dared to aim higher, to break barriers, to reach for the stars, to make the unknown known. We count these moments as our proudest achievements. But we lost all that. And perhaps we've just forgotten that we are still pioneers and we've barely begun. And that are greatest accomplishments cannot be behind us, as our destiny lies above us."[67]

Read that voice-over material, the last paragraph, again.

Every image that accompanies this trailer is of White people: struggling to survive, to live; fighting to grow and sustain the next generation; understanding that limitation of the imagination is a recipe for destitution and failure.

It looks like a trailer directly from the studios of the Third Reich, propaganda for a people resolute in their greatness and resolved to move forward.

Simply put, it's a glorification of White people.

Juxtapose that with these words from *Narratives and Spaces: Technology and the Construction of American Culture*, Dave Nye's book. He describes Black attitudes to the White man's lunar (loony?) mission:

The Apollo Program was most appreciated by those who were young, affluent, well-educated, Caucasian, and male.

---

[67] Jagernauth, "Watch: First Trailer."

The space program seemed justified by the knowledge gained and by the improved commodities "spun-off" as by-products, such as food concentrates, Teflon, and computer miniaturization. The Los Angeles Herald-Examiner made a characteristic list in an editorial: "America's moon program has benefited mankind. It has brought better color television, water purification at less cost, new paints and plastics, improved weather forecasting, medicine, respirators, walkers for the handicapped, laser surgery, world-wide communications, new transportation systems, earthquake predictions systems and solar power."

People in poverty evidently did not believe that things such as solar power or new plastics would benefit them more than direct spending on social programs. The stronger opposition lay within the black community, where less than one in four people supported the expenditure of $4 billion a year for the Apollo Program. A minority added, "God never intended us to go into space." . . . most black newspapers carried editorials and cartoons attacking the space program, including the Chicago Daily Defender and Muhammad Speaks. The New York Amsterdam News cartoon depicted President Richard Nixon smiling up at the moon while sitting on a huge spherical bomb with a lighted fuse, labeled, "minority frustrations." The accompanying editorial attacked the "outlandish costs of the space race," and declared that, "Man can conquer space, yes. But man has still to conquer his homeland. And that's where the real action is, brother."

In July of 1969 on the eve of Apollo XI, the Poor People's Campaign came to Cape Kennedy. To emphasize the slow pace of change, 150 people arrived in wagons pulled by mules. They both protested that the launch was taking place, and, perhaps incongruously, demanded 40 VIP passes to see it close-up. The Reverend Ralph Abernathy urged NASA administrator Dr. Thomas Paine to convert his technology to find new ways to feed the poor. Pained promised to see if food concentrates developed for space could be adapted to feed the undernourished on earth. Paine gave them VIP passes, and declared that the space program was compatible with the war on poverty: "I want you to hitch your wagon to our rocket and tell the people the NASA program is an example of what this country can do." Paine was attempting to harness the old metaphor, "hitch your wagon to a star." But try to visualize what could happen to a wooden wagon hitched to a Saturn V rocket at blast-off. Perhaps African-American views are best encapsulated by a contrast. Duke Ellington, whose music represented an older generation, performed for ABC's national audience a new song, "Moon Maiden," to mark the event. But when the successful moon landing was announced to 50,000 African-Americans at a soul concert in Harlem, many booed.[68]

Booed.

Sadly, no one dares *boo* at the conditions of majority Black cities, like 83 percent Black Detroit. Instead, the GOP and people like Rand Paul believe we should practice outreach there, to a people who took the money that should have gone to space exploration and turned it into Detroit (a powerful glimpse at what the War on Poverty bought us).

Oh, but it gets better:

Many black papers questioned the use of American funds for space research at a time when many African Americans were struggling at the margins of the working class. An editorial in the *Los Angeles Sentinel,* for example, argued against Apollo in no uncertain terms, saying, "It would appear that the fathers of our nation would allow a few thousand hungry people to die for the lack of a few thousand dollars while they would contaminate the moon and its sterility for the sake of 'progress' and spend billions of dollars in the process, while people are hungry, ill-clothed, poorly educated (if at all)."

This is, of course, a complicated story. When 200 black protesters marched on Cape Canaveral to protest the launch

---

[68] Nye, *Narratives and Spaces*, 151–2.

of Apollo 14, one Southern Christian Leadership Conference
leader claimed, "America is sending lazy white boys to the
moon because all they're doing is looking for moon rocks. If
there was work to be done, they'd send a nigger."[69]

Odd choice of words from the member of Martin Luther King's
SCLC, considering the unbelievable amount of work "lazy
white boys" put into engineering the Apollo craft that took
whitey to the Moon (while a "rat done bit my sister Nell").

Oh, but it gets even better than that. Courtesy of Gerard
DeGroot's book, *Dark Side of the Moon: The Magnificent Madness of the American Lunar Quest*, we learn that Abernathy
believed the gap between the different races of mankind was
far greater than the gap between the Earth and the Moon:

> Space was a dominating issue of the 1960s; civil rights was
> another. The two were distinctly separate: space showcased
> the country's achievement; civil rights underlined her short-
> coming. The two issues did nevertheless intersect, most of-
> ten when civil rights campaigners argued that the billions
> required to put a few men into orbit could be better utilized
> to help millions of blacks onto their feet. On the eve of the
> Apollo 11 launch, the activist Ralph Abernathy argued that:
>   "A society that can resolve to conquer space; to put man
> in a place where in ages past it was considered only God
> could reach; to appropriate vast billions; to systematically
> set about to discover the necessary scientific knowledge;
> that society deserves both acclaim for achievement and con-
> tempt for bizarre social values. For though it has the capac-
> ity to meet extraordinary challenges, it has failed to use its
> ability to rid itself of the scourges of racism, poverty and
> war, all of which were brutally scarring the nation even as
> it mobilized for the assault on the solar system." Why is it
> less exciting to the human spirit to enlarge man by making
> him brother to his fellow man? There is more distance be-
> tween the races of man than between the moon and the

---

[69] Madrigal, "Moondoggle."

earth. To span the vastness of human space is ultimately more glorious than any other achievement."

Abernathy's complaint reached a crescendo when he led a march of perhaps three hundred followers from the Poor People's Campaign to the Apollo 11 launch site. A light rain was falling as his army approached. A number of mules, symbols of rural poverty, were in the van, proving a stark contrast to the massive, high-tech Saturn rocket. Abernathy stopped, then gave a short speech to a crowd of onlookers who had the Moon on their mind. He pointed out that one-fifth of the nation lacked adequate food, clothing, shelter, and medical care and that, given such deep poverty, space flight seemed inhuman. The crowd remained polite, but most of the spectators wanted this spoilsport to get out of the way so that show could start.

Abernathy was met by Tom Paine who had by his side, appropriately, Julian Scheer, NASA's public information officer. Paine's presence was carefully engineered to suggest that NASA took the plight of the poor seriously, even if it could do nothing to alleviate that suffering. He explained that he was himself a member of the NAACP and sensitive to the struggle of poor blacks. But he told Abernathy (and the assembled crowd) "if we could solve the problems of poverty by not pushing the button to launch men to the Moon tomorrow, then we would not push that button.[70]

In some different dimension, a very different button was pushed by White America; not just the one that sent the Apollo 11 mission to the Moon, but (after the Black riots in the 1960s left Detroit, Newark, Watts, and other major cities in ruins) put in motion a plan to repatriate Black people back to Africa.

Abernathy was right when he said: "There is more distance between the races of man than between the moon and the earth. To span the vastness of human space is ultimately more glorious than any other achievement."[71]

---

[70] DeGroot, *Dark Side of the Moon*, 234.
[71] Quoted in Ibid.

However, since America went down the path of funding every civil rights initiative and abandoning space, we have seen trillions upon trillions of dollars (as well as untold opportunity costs and lost equity) go toward eliminating the racial gap in every measurable category where Blacks fail and Whites succeed.

Looking at Detroit in 2013, spanning the vastness of human space (and bridging the racial gap in achievement) and finding a way to navigate the distance between the White race and Black race is a path we should have never, ever have tried to go down.

23

"Like a Step on the Moon": How a DWL
Explains the Election of Barack Obama

September 18th, 2012

You wait and you wait and you wait for that perfect quote to be uttered from the lips of Disingenuous White Liberal (DWL) that encapsulates their entire philosophy, just so you finally can understand the driving force behind their actions.

And when it is finally supplied, all you can do is laugh. Courtesy of the Academy Award-winning composer Randy Newman, we now are offered insight into the penetrating mind of the DWL:

Randy Newman is weighing in on the presidential election, and he's playing the race card through a song he wrote called "I'm Dreaming."

The piano tune features the refrain: "I'm dreaming of a white president." It is full of satirical, sarcastic—and signature—Newman anecdotes about someone who votes for the president because he is white.

Newman, who is white, is openly supporting President Barack Obama. He says he wants the public to find comedic relief in the song, but to also know he's serious about his thoughts that racism is well and alive in the world—and in the current presidential race. He called racism "the great issue of this country."

"I felt that that sentiment exists in the country," Newman said in an interview Monday. "I don't know how many
people you can get to admit it. I think maybe zero."

Newman believes Obama will be re-elected in November
and feels that Republican contender Mitt Romney isn't a "serious candidate for president."

Newman said he's proud of how America has progressed,
though, but adds that "there's a long way to go."

"No European country would have elected a black man,"
he said. "I can't believe it happened. I think it's fantastic,
like a step on the moon."[72]

"Like a step on the Moon?"

It would be difficult to ascertain what Newman means by
"how America has progressed," but a cursory glance at Detroit
and Birmingham in the post-civil rights era wouldn't be pru-
dent for one professing "progress" as synonymous with Black
rule.

But no matter: it's the act itself that Mr. Newman supports,
damn the consequences. For Mr. Newman, supporting Obama
is a liberating experience as it frees him from being called either racist or a White supremacist (which all White people are
in the eyes of non-Whites, which is why DWLs place that community's promotion as the great possible outcome in any endeavor).

But comparing the election of a Black man to the office of
President of the United States to "a step on the moon?" Seems
outlandish, right?

Considering it was Black people who complained that the
Apollo mission wasted money that would have been better
spent, not on sending White people to the Moon, but on keeping
White people grounded to the reality of eternally caring for the
Black Undertow.

It is in "Live from the Moon: The Societal Impact of Apollo"
by Andrew Chaikin, a chapter in the book *Societal Impact of*

---

[72] Fekadu, "Randy Newman writes."

Spaceflight, that the Black/White view of space exploration comes into view. There is no grey in this discussion:

As momentous as Apollo 8 was, its historical impact was equaled, even surpassed, by that of Apollo 11, the first land‐ing of humans on another world. When Neil Armstrong and Buzz Aldrin took history's first moonwalk on 20 July 1969, an estimated 600 million people—one‐fifth of the world's population—witnessed it on live television and radio. it was difficult not to feel the enormity of the event, and some ob‐servers viewed it as a turning point in the course of civiliza‐tion—especially science fiction writers, many of whom had envisioned the event in the decades before it happened. One was Robert Heinlein, who had penned the story for the 1950 film Destination Moon; on the day of the moonwalk he ap‐peared as a guest on CBS news' television coverage of the mission. "This is the greatest event in all the history of the human race up to this time, "Heinlein said. "Today is New Year's Day of the Year one. If we don't change the calendar, historians will do so."

And yet no one could ignore the fact that the first Moon landing, taking place at a time of continuing turmoil in the United States, was also evoking dissent. On the day before the Apollo 11 launch, Ralph Abernathy, chairman of the Southern Christian Leadership council, came to the Ken‐nedy Space Center with a small group of protesters to draw attention to the plight of the nation's poor. And in New York City on the day of the landing, a member of Harlem's black community voiced the same concern to a network TV re‐porter:

"The cash they wasted, as far as I'm concerned, in getting to the moon, could have been used to feed poor black people in Harlem, and all over this country. So, you know, never mind the moon; let's get some of that cash in Harlem."

A defense of the Apollo expenditures (the estimated total was $24 billion) came from Arthur C. Clarke, the writer and futurist who had collaborated with director Stanley Kubrick to create the screenplay for Kubrick's 1968 epic science fiction film *2001: A Space Odyssey*. In his comments, Clarke looked to Apollo's long-term benefits:

"I think in the long run the money that's been put into the space program is one of the best investments this country has ever made . . . This is a downpayment on the future of mankind. It's as simple as that." [. . .]

By winning the space race with the Soviet Union, Apollo had given a boost to the nation's prestige in the world and, for many Americans, a heightened a sense of national pride. But seen through another lens, particularly that of the nation's disadvantaged, the view was starkly different. To black poet Gil Scott-Heron, Apollo was emblematic of the nation's racial inequalities. He expressed this in "Whitey on the Moon," which begins,

"A rat done bit my sister Nell.
(with Whitey on the moon)
Her face and arms began to swell.
(and Whitey's on the moon)
I can't pay no doctor bill (but Whitey's on the moon)
Ten years from now I'll be payin' still.
(while Whitey's on the moon)."[73]

No, Mr. Heinlein, historians didn't start the calendar over. That would have to wait until January 20th, 2009, when Mr. Obama was elected President of the United States, at least in the eyes of Mr. Newman.

The exploration of space effectively ended: we could have been on Mars, but instead we funded Black-Run America. Because we chose the latter path, Mr. Newman and DWLs like him can feel morally superior to the rest of us. Had we chosen the former path, we would have felt superior to everyone else as we prepared to traverse the stars.

---

[73] Dick and Launius, *Societal Impact of Spaceflight*, 625.

Now, we must use GPS devices to steer us clear of Black ghettos, largely funded by the money that would have propelled us to the stars.

Never forget what Lawrence Auster wrote:

WHAT BLACKS CONTRIBUTE TO CIVILIZATION

Did you know this? I didn't. I just came upon it in Wikipedia's article on Ralph Abernathy, Martin Luther King's successor as the head of the Southern Christian Leadership Conference:

"On the eve of the Apollo 11 launch, July 15, 1969, Abernathy arrived at Cape Canaveral with several hundred members of the poor people to protest spending of government space exploration, while many Americans remained poor. He was met by Thomas O. Paine, the Administrator of NASA, whom he told that in the face of such suffering, space flight represented an inhuman priority and funds should be spent instead to "feed the hungry, clothe the naked, tend the sick, and house the homeless." Mr. Paine told Abernathy that the advances in space exploration were child's play compared to the tremendously difficult human problems of society, and told him that "if we could solve the problems of poverty by not pushing the button to launch men to the moon tomorrow, then we would not push that button." On the day of the launch, Dr. Abernathy led a small group of protesters to the restricted guest viewing area of the space center and chanted, "We are not astronauts, but we are people."

So there you have it. One of the greatest achievements in history, the first manned flight to the Moon, and the most prestigious black civil rights organization, the SCLC, *wanted it not to take place*, because they thought the money it cost could be better spent on transfer payments to blacks. And that is all that blacks as an organized community have to contribute to our civilization: endless complaints about white injustice to blacks, and endless demands for the wealth and goods that white people have produced, and that

blacks are incapable of producing. Plus a third "contribution" not brought out in this incident: endless threats of violence and riots if the blacks don't get their way.

The black blackmail and dragging down of white civilization will continue, until whites stand up, name it for what it
is, and say, "No more."

But since there is zero indication that whites will do that
in any foreseeable future (to the contrary, as we can see in
the George Zimmerman affair, whites, including many "con-
servatives," are becoming more, not less attuned to the
worldview of "Black-Run America"), the black blackmail and
dragging down of our civilization will continue and inten-
sify, until the civilization is ruined.[74]

Progress.

---

[74] Auster, "What Blacks Contribute."

24

Too Black to Fail, Part II: 83 Percent Black Detroit Getting $100 Million from Federal Government to Fight Blight

April 16th, 2014

Detroit is 83 percent Black.

Since 1974, blacks have been in control of the executive branch of government in the city, working to rewrite rules on contracting to ensure connected Black-owned firms get preferential treatment (racial cronyism); with White flight from a city that was more than 80 percent white in 1950, Detroit has regressed to the Black mean.

The city in 2014 has been remade in a Black image, the collective achievement not of liberals, progressives, Democrats, or unions, but Black individuals.

Dreams very different from the one Martin Luther King talked about in 1963 built Detroit; the implementation of his dream tore the civilization Whites built in Detroit apart. More than 80,000 abandoned buildings serve as a reminder that a very different people built the city than currently occupy it, with the housing stock that once sheltered White families rotting and crumbling under Black rule.

Never forget America abandoned our mission to investigate the heavens, instead embarking on a costly adventure to perpetually engage in *Waiting for "Superman"* to close the racial gap in learning/achievement.

He's never coming.

But Detroit is too Black to fail. Though the failure of the city under Black rule should be a critical blow to the crucial mission of uplifting Blacks, it must continue unabated:

> The White House and city of Detroit are in talks in recent days to free up to $100 million in federal blight funding that could indirectly soften the blow of pension fund cuts and other financial issues for the Motor City.
>
> No deal has been reached and the Obama administration has been eager to emphasize it will not provide a bailout for Detroit. But as mediators, the city and its pension funds have worked to reach a deal to help speed the city's exit from its record-setting Chapter 9 bankruptcy, the federal government's additional blight funding could allow the city's emergency manager, Kevyn Orr, to redirect some of his planned blight spending toward pensions and other priorities.
>
> The Obama administration would potentially allow the state of Michigan to redirect "Hardest Hit" funds that are earmarked to prevent foreclosure to blight removal—as it did in August—but officials emphasize that none of the funds would be spent directly to fund retiree pensions or be used by the state or city general fund.
>
> Orr has proposed spending $500 million over 10 years to combat the city's tens of thousands of abandoned buildings and blighted structures. Detroit has an estimated 78,000 blighted and abandoned properties and the federal government has helped fund a comprehensive survey of the entire city to better track the blight problems.
>
> Officials involved in the talks emphasize that tentative deals reached with the pensions that would include a 4.5 percent cut in retiree benefits from non-public safety pension recipients are not contingent on the Obama administration putting money into the blight program.[75]

Too Black to fail. But why the blight?

---

[75] Shepardson, "Detroit, feds talk up."

Why couldn't Black people, who inherited a city with all the infrastructure already completed, be unable to sustain it?

Could it be because the 95 percent Black Detroit Public School system produced the "lowest scores ever recorded in the twenty-one-year history of the national math proficiency tests"? [76]

The Detroit Public Schools posted the worst scores on record in the most recent test of students in large central U.S. cities.

The scores came on the Trial Urban District Assessment, a national test developed by the Governing Board, the National Center for Education Statistics of the U.S. Department of Education and the Council of the Great City Schools.

The test for urban districts is part of the National Assessment of Educational Progress test given to school districts nationwide.

"There is no jurisdiction of any kind, at any level, at any time in the 30-year history of NAEP that has ever registered such low numbers," said Michael Casserly, executive director of the Council on Great City Schools, a Washington, D.C.-based coalition of urban school districts.

"They are barely above what one would expect simply by chance, as if the kids simply guessed at the answers," he said. [77]

Civilizations aren't built by guessing. That's how they are destroyed.

Back in 1969, on the day the Apollo 11 crew would be launched into space, the agenda for the United States of America was set by Black people utilizing a horse and buggy to make their point—all in the shadow of the greatest vessel for exploration and true progress ever pieced together by man.

---

[76] Winerip, "For Detroit Schools."
[77] Beene, "Detroit's public schools."

Kenneth Lipartito and Orville R. Butler's book, *A History of the Kennedy Space Center*, makes clear that on the day mankind would watch three White men rocket into space on a mission to the Moon, Black people would use horse-drawn carriages to protest the launch.

A misallocation of funds, with the teeming Black masses a more appropriate expenditure than a foolish lunar mission. Lipartito and Butler write:

The entire earth was experiencing its own moonshot madness. A man in Tokyo was going to mark the occasion in a hotel room wearing a space suit and eating "astronaut food" for the duration of the mission. Buddhists worshipped at shrines resembling the Apollo ship. And a few miles south of the launch site at the town of Cocoa, another gathering was taking place.

Five hundred marchers from the Poor People's Campaign led by civil rights activists Hosea Williams and Ralph Abernathy had converged on the Cape. With America spending some $24 billion to send a handful of men to the moon, they asked, how could the nation not afford to tackle poverty at home? Edward Kennedy, brother of the president who had started it all, called for putting earth needs such as "poverty, hunger, pollution and housing" ahead of space."

Protestors from the Poor People's Campaign held an all-night vigil as the countdown proceeded. The next day, they marched behind two mule-drawn wagons, a reminder that poverty lingered among many African Americans. Abernathy and forty of his contingent received VIP badges and seats in the viewing stands at KSC. The remaining protestors started a slow trek toward the Center. "We do not oppose the moon shot," declared Hosea Williams. "Our purpose is to protest America's inability to choose human priorities." "We're wishing the astronauts all good luck,"

Abernathy added. "But we think attention should be given to poor people too."[78]

---

[78] Butler and Lipartito, *History of the Kennedy Space Center*, 15–6.

We chose those "human priorities" Williams touted, abandoned the Moon, Mars, and space exploration.

We got Detroit instead.

25

"The Dream" After 50 Years: You Can't Wake Up from the Nightmare Until You Find the Courage to Renounce the Guilt and Embrace the Privilege

August 28th, 2013

Jules Verne had a dream.
Arthur C. Clarke had a dream.
Carl Sagan had a dream.
Robert Heinlein had a dream.
Werner Von Braun had a dream.
Ever since man first gazed into the night sky and saw millions of lights glaring back, the dream has been to find what's out there, and perhaps discover if anyone's looking back on a distant world wondering the same thing.

The Post Standard, based in Syracuse, New York, published a fitting epitaph to a long-dead civilization on July 17th, 1969. Under the title "Poor Give Reminder of Earth's Ills," the Associated Press reported:

A gigantic moon rocket and an old mule-drawn wagon wrote a paradox of humanity Wednesday.

While the Apollo 11 thundered toward the moon as a thrilling step in the conquest of space, a contingent of the Poor People's Campaign trudged a highway far below—as a reminder of hunger and poverty yet unconquered on earth.

"We must have a launching of a program against poverty—hunger in particular—racism and war; a launching that is just as effective and beautiful as was the moonshot launching," said the Rev. Ralph David Abernathy, leader of the Poor People's group that had VIP seats for the rocket spectacular.

Abernathy and 45 followers watched from choice seats at Kennedy Space Center while another contingent of his antipoverty corps briefly blocked traffic on a highway to the center.

About 40 marchers, trailed by a two-mule wagon, walked along the causeway from the space center and onto U.S. 1 before dispersing and boarding buses.

At the VIP viewing site—separate from that where Vice President Spiro Agnew, former President Lyndon B. Johnson and other dignitaries were—Abernathy and his group sang "freedom songs" and he spoke to the entire crowd before the launch. He said he'd come to see the spaceshot and to "demonstrate and protest that America has mixed up her priorities." While the Apollo moon-landing voyage was the culmination of 10 years work, he said, "this nation still needs to plan a program for meeting human needs." Abernathy, president of the Southern Christian Leadership Conference and successor to the late Dr. Martin Luther King Jr., called on the spectators to join the antipoverty campaign. He was busy signing autographs until about five minutes before the launch. After the Apollo roared away, Abernathy and his group sang, "We Shall Overcome," the civil rights theme song.

Three days later, men—White men—would step foot on the Moon, courtesy of technological advances and courage seemingly written into the DNA of Western Man.

Imagine the juxtaposition of the gigantic Apollo rocket in Cape Canaveral, next to a mule-drawn wagon, which only a century prior was one of the primary means of transporting White settlers across the American continent.

For the fulfillment of Manifest Destiny.

Yet, in the entire history of any African people, no evidence is available that the invention of the wheel ever occurred.

But Martin Luther King Jr. had his dream, and anyone else who ever dared, perchance to dream, saw them go up in a cloud of righteous smoke.

And thus, the genesis of what we have labeled Manifest Destruction was born.

Had MLK not been assassinated, he'd have led this Poor People's March on Cape Canaveral; he'd have been the one serenading the crowd with the Negro spiritual "We Shall Overcome" as a massive rocket, built by thousands of White men, hurdled three White men into the heavens.

America did launch a program against poverty and racism, scrapping the dreams of science fiction writers and visionaries in favor of a Black man's dream, whose only goal was to ensure Black people took power in cities like Detroit, Baltimore, Washington D.C., Atlanta, Memphis, and Birmingham.

The movement MLK led aimed to ensure a massive transfer of wealth and morality transpired, marooning the White man on this earth with the teeming masses using something called "White privilege" as a rope to restrain his spirit.

But it will break.

For in the above AP article from 1969 rests the comical reality of evolution, and in 2013, we have the devolution of our major cities from hubs of commerce and growth to the blighted remnants of a failed civilization.

The civilization of MLK and Abernathy, where we abandoned the pursuit of space exploration and decided to ameliorate poverty and racism.

Think about that: in ten years' time, men in the 1960s set forth to put a man on the Moon by the end of the decade; since then, we have seen an endless pursuit of eradicating inequality in the name of justice, under a banner with a picture of Comrade MLK.

All we have to show for it is Detroit.

And Gary (Indiana).

And Baltimore.

Newark and Camden, New Jersey too.

But on Earth's natural satellite is a reminder of not only what could have been, because the physical evidence for genetic inequality rests more than a hundred thousand miles away forever a silent guard to racial differences.

A footprint.

Man stood on the Moon.

White man.

What is the Black man's footprint on this world?

What is the legacy of MLK's dream, which Abernathy carried on and kept alive by singing Negro Spirituals as the Apollo spacecraft roared into the heavens?

Detroit in 2013.

No, the last fifty years were not a dream.

You can't wake up from the nightmare until you find the courage to renounce the guilt and embrace the privilege.

26

Why is MLK's Dream the Only Road Map for the Future of America?

August 25th, 2013

Fifty years ago today, America was less than six years away from sending men to the Moon.

Detroit was still one of America' most important cities, with a population of 1.8 million people that was 72 percent White.

Today, Detroit is 82 percent Black, a bankrupt city where more than fifty thousand dogs aimlessly roam the streets.

Streets that were paved with only one ingredient in mind during their construction: fulfilling Martin Luther King Jr.'s dream.

Today, tens of thousands of Black people converged on Washington D.C. to "march again" in honor of MLK and the desire to keep alive his "dream."

Never mind that it came true in Detroit.

There's still work to do, Attorney General Eric Holder said in his speech from the steps of the Lincoln Memorial in 2013.[79]

Though Birmingham, Alabama is a 74 percent Black city (complete with Black mayor, Black police chief, and majority Black city council), we still must wonder if MLK's dream is a reality. That's what the Birmingham News actually published, thus begging the question "what exactly was his dream?"[80]

---

[79] Office of Public Affairs, "Attorney General Eric Holder."
[80] AP, "Is Martin Luther King."

MLK III, the eldest son of Martin Luther King himself, said "the task is still not done," when he spoke that same day, again begging the simple question: what the hell was Martin Luther King's dream and why in the world is it the only approved dream Americans must all embrace as the vision of the future?[81]

Had Martin Luther King Jr. not been assassinated in 1968, he'd have joined his right-hand man Ralph Abernathy in 1969 when the latter protested the monumental waste of money White America was expending in reaching to the stars (for a glimpse of the real King, read the *Playboy* interview from January 1965).

In Mark Thompson's "Space Race: African American Newspapers Respond to Sputnik and Apollo 11," he makes clear that Rev. Abernathy—MLK's successor to the mantle of number one racial huckster and new head of his Southern Christian Leadership Conference (SCLC)—and much of Black America didn't share their White countrymen's enthusiasm for space exploration:

> Before the launch, civil rights activist Rev. Ralph D. Abernathy led a protest complaining about the amount of money spent on the Apollo program while vast numbers of people remained at the poverty level. "America has reached out to the stars but has not reached out to her starving poor," explained Abernathy while leading a small group of 15 African Americans through the Cape Kennedy Visitors Center.
>
> An article penned by Booker Griffin in the *Los Angeles Sentinel* proffered the argument that while the moon landing was definitely "one of the miracles of the ages" and that "[t]aken at face value, it would seem that all Americans would rejoice at such a monumental occurrence," Griffin announced: "I do not." In Griffin's article, entitled "Moon Dust and Black Disgust," a central theme was the contrast between what the Apollo program achieved and what

---

[81] AP, "Marching for King's dream."

remained underachieved on earth in the black communities: "Here is a country that cannot pass a rat control bill to protect black babies from rats, but can spend billions to explore rocks, craters and dust thousands of miles away."[82]

In 2013, after forty years of Black political control of Detroit, much of the city is now nothing more than rocks and dust, with burnt-out buildings a reminder that some form of civilization once flourished in the city: White civilization.

We could have been on Mars, but we terminated that mission in exchange for seeing Martin Luther King's dream come to fruition.

It's time to tear up that roadmap for the future.

Judging by 2013 Detroit and Birmingham, there's more promise for civilization amid the dust, rocks, and craters of the Moon, then in these two Black politically (and morally) controlled municipalities.

For $20, you can buy an acre of land on the Moon.[83] For $1, you can buy a house in 82 percent Black Detroit.[84]

That, my friends, is Martin Luther King's dream come true—in monetary value.

[82] Thompson, "Space Race," 52.
[83] See The Lunar Registry website
[84] Knowles, "Forsaken Detroit homes."

27

"It Will Silently Mock Whatever America Becomes in 2034": A Flag on Moon and Its Future in the Comedy Business

June 13th, 2014

The Trenton Public School System (New Jersey) is 95.9 percent Black or Hispanic.[85]

And because of the irresponsible breeding habits of their parents, these 95.9 percent Black or Hispanic students are basically wards of an increasingly—but still funded by Whites—non-White state.

Free breakfast.

Free lunch.

And now free dinner:

City children attending after-school programs will be offered free, hot meals for dinner starting in the fall. Aramark, which has the contract for food service in the city schools, currently offers free breakfast and lunch to students enrolled in the city's public schools.

Aramark General Manager Francisca Sohl said as long as educational after-school programs are offered, students attending will be eligible for the free meal. "These are home-style hot meals," said Sohl. Menu items will include chicken Parmesan made with whole wheat pasta, green beans, meat loaf and collard greens.

---

[85] Perry, "Opinion: Health of Trenton."

"This is going to go a long way for our kids in Trenton," said board member Sasa Olessi-Montano, who added that many students go home to no dinner or a meal that is not nutritious. Sohl said the plan is to slowly roll out the program so it is offered in all 22 city schools by the end of next school year.

The rollout will begin with elementary and middle schools in October and December. Aramark does not charge Trenton students because the majority of students in the district are low-income and qualify for free lunches. The food programs are funded by federal grants.[86]

On July 16th, 1969, the United States of America had two potential paths to go down for the future. We were launching the Apollo 11 mission to the Moon, meaning the stars was one destination. The other was typified by the Poor People's Campaign, led by Rev. Ralph Abernathy, who demanded we cease funding the adventure to the heavens and instead fund—well, what's going on in 95.9 percent Black or Hispanic Trenton Public Schools in 2014.

Seriously.

Trenton Public Schools in 2014, with free meals for non-White children, is exactly the route America decided on for the future.

Hosea Williams, a leader of the Southern Christian Leadership Conference that organized the Poor People's Campaign, was quoted as saying on July 16th, 1969:

This woman gets $82 a month and a one-room shack. Why should we be worrying about sending three men to the moon where here are 10 people dying of starvation? If we can spend $100 a mile to send three men to the moon, can't we, for God's sake, feed our hungry?[87]

---

86 Pizzi, "Aramark to offer Trenton."
87 Perry, "For the Poor People's Campaign."

A couple letters to the editor in the October 1969 issue of *Ebony* magazine should help anyone with a brain understand what those three White men going to the Moon meant to Black people:

I'd proudly give an arm or leg to be able to cheer Apollo 11 like the white folks on America's globe. What I would not give to stand on the sea shore *[sic]* of Cape Kennedy waving the astronauts home with the country's flag, red, white, blue. What's more, I'd like to stand tall and erect as an American citizen bowing gracefully (as if in the presence of a queen or king) to those three men who have played their roles excellent. I'd like to scream from the top of my voice uttering these words, "Another victory to the United States of America, the greatest country in the world!"

But as a black as I am, I dare not cheer some $92.5 billion up in the sky when my black brothers and sisters, the children of Ethiopia, Ghana, Mali, Nigeria and other countries of the mother land *[sic]*, starve for food, wishing for the disappearance of ghettos, and for economic stability and better educational and employment opportunities.

Doris Rutledge
Student, Miles College
Birmingham, Ala.

The Moon landing was a historical first in world events. Many people in this country watched their TV sets with a great sense of pride.

How magnificent it must have been to see the entire operation being carried out by someone who could have been you, your brother, your son, or more importantly, your father.

Imagine a child's bright eyes if he could say, "My dad is doing the countdown. My dad is one of the astronauts. That's my dad at the computer. My dad is at Houston Mission Control."

A sense of pride is certainly proper and fitting. And those who identify best with the people chosen to carry out this mission, must now have egos at least as high as the Moon.

Do I identify best? I saw no one who looked like me, nor my brother, nor my son, nor my father. For I am black, and so are they.

Nona E. Smith
Harlem, NY

Funny—I don't identify with the community of Trenton for the same reason Nona E. Smith couldn't find anything worth taking pride in in the Apollo 11 mission. Just as the mission involved almost no Black faces (maybe a janitor or two at Cape Canaveral), Trenton Public Schools are filled with students from K-12 who I can't identify with at all.

You see, Black people's mark on America is found in the blight of formerly thriving urban areas of the country. The conditions White people created long ago in places like Detroit, Chicago, Trenton, Newark, Camden, Philadelphia, Baltimore, Rochester, New York City, Gary, Cleveland, Buffalo, and Milwaukee attracted Black people from the south who migrated to these cities and, in the span of only a few generations, remade them in their image.

Tho' much is taken, much abides.

The glory once found in these cities can still be seen if one looks hard enough; the glory of the accomplishment of July 20th, 1969, when two White men stepped onto the Moon, is a fact all eyes must consider when they look upon the Earth's natural satellite.

White men, and only White men, have gone there.

Walked there.

And looked back at the earth from there, realizing how tiny our home is when framed by the vastness of the universe.

Wherever the Black sons and daughters of the Great Migration have gone, conditions like those found in Newark, New Jersey to Detroit, Michigan are a hallmark of this trek.

And though Rev. Abernathy's hopes and vision for the future have come true for now, the flag of a people scarcely represented among the student body of the Trenton Public School system in 2014 stands resolute on the Moon.

Silently mocking the decision to embark on the Poor People's Crusade as national policy.

I was asked to consider what America 2034 will look like for the online publication *American Renaissance*. Though I harbor no optimism for America's fate, every time I see the Moon (be it during the day or when I look up into the night sky), I immediately smile: our fate isn't to be assimilated into the ruins of Detroit, or to smile knowing our kids can eat on the taxpayer dime in Trenton.

There is no great awakening coming, or political or spiritual revival nearing to save America; we hitched our wagon to the Poor People's Crusade instead of the goal of the Apollo program.

There's no going back, but there will come a moment when the crusade of Rev. Abernathy runs off a cliff; and then it's over.

Most people are incapable of understanding the American experiment has already ended, believing instead to hold on to some Norman Rockwell vestige of the past as a sign something great is only just around the corner.

There's only Trenton.

There's only Detroit.

But if you look up, preferably on a crystal-clear night sky, you'll see the Moon.

Smile when you look at it.

Your people didn't create the conditions of 2014 Trenton.

Your people didn't create the conditions of 2014 Detroit.

Your people did land on the Moon.

Those peddling the hoax we didn't land on the Moon as fact embrace the type of egalitarian mindset shared by those who pin all hope on uplifting the Black and brown populations of the world on the White man's pocketbook.

Money can't alter genetics.

Not even a blank check.

As I wrote back in 2009, I don't view the collapse of the American Experiment as a bad thing. I was born into a world where our country's future was already hitched to a wooden mule cart, piloted by Rev. Abernathy's stern hope to keep our eyes off the heavens.[88]

And it was at a very young age I realized something was incongruent with the population occupying our major cities and the one that landed on the Moon.

And though, starting in 2014, the 95.9 percent black or Hispanic Trenton Public School system will enjoy three free meals a day, when they look up at the Moon, an incomprehensible alien whisper will mock them.

Just as it will silently mock whatever America becomes in 2034.

From the article I wrote in 2009, I'd like to pull out this paragraph. It's not of my own pen, but something I reflect upon daily:

> When a state is dying, one dies with it only to the extent that one is psychologically and spiritually a part of it. Those who are a part of it—the vast majority—will perish with it. Those who are not—the tiny minority—will not, and some of them will survive as carriers of life. The only disaster, once the state is dying, would be prolongation by some artificial means of support.[89]

The country that gave birth to Trenton in 2014 is not the same one that gave birth to the people capable of flying to the Moon with a slide rule as their guide in 1969.

---

[88] Kersey, "Prospects for Racial Separation."
[89] Quoted in Ibid., 70.

28

"We Have Pretty Much Dismantled Our Civilization in an Effort to Accommodate Blacks"

May 31st, 2014

The great story of our time is one hidden in plain sight.

On the day we—"we" meaning White men, birthed by White women—launched Apollo 11 into the heavens, Blacks demanded the money spent on the program be diverted to them.

Simeon Booker, longtime writer for *Jet* magazine, wrote this editorial in the July 31st, 1969 edition.

Read it.

Memorize it.

Landing a man on the Moon and beginning the conquest/colonization of space meant nothing to Blacks, who instead believed the money spent on such a mission should go to them.

And only them:

Moon Probe Laudable—But Blacks Need Help

Landing an astronaut on the moon has more priority in America than putting a black man on his feet, in a job, or a poor family on a decent diet. This space accomplishment at a cost of billions of dollars will receive coast to coast acclaim and international attention.

But as a black Washington correspondent, I see this week as a crucial period in history. There will be headlines and hours of radio and television time on the day to day activity. President Nixon invited the president of his alma mater, Whittier College, to speak at the White House religious

service on "the Meaning of The Man on The Moon." Meanwhile what of the man in the street—in poverty stricken Ap-
palachia, Watts, and Harlem. He wished the astronauts well
and marvels at their courage.

But he also wonders if the powers of science and technology will ever focus in such a fashion on his problems. Thanks
to modern communications, even the simplest ghetto
dweller knows that the American space program and its
counterpart in the Soviet Union are almost as political in
their motives as they are scientific.

And while the victims of poverty watch the space race
with awe, we wonder how long it will be before the hypnosis
of a moon flight wears off and the victims of poverty realize
that they are still hungry. Perhaps the presence of the mule
train of the Poor People's Campaign at Cape Kennedy will
remind some people that their NASA tax dollars might best
be spent in other ways.

Sometime, somehow, we Americans—and the Russians
as well—must think about making the earth a better place
to live. To escape to the moon is no answer for any of us—
black, white, brown or yellow.[90]

Reading this editorial only a day after the "poet" Maya Angelou
passed away helped me realize what we lost when we embarked on a mission of uplifting Black people instead of launching a mission to Mars.

John Derbyshire, writing at *VDARE*, put it quite succinctly
when he nailed America's mission over the past fifty years
(sadly, started five years before the Moon landing on July 20th,
1969).

He wrote:

For fifty years now we've been giving breaks to blacks, and
not just Affirmative Action sinecures like those enjoyed by
Ta-Nehisi Coates and the late, but equally talentless, Ms.
Angelou.

---

[90] Simeon Booker, editorial comment, *Jet Magazine,* July 31, 1969.

We abolished federal Civil Service exams because blacks couldn't pass them. Our colleges turn away nonblack kids so that less well-qualified blacks can be admitted.

We shower public money on bogus claimants to farm-loan discrimination. Our media observe exquisitely sensitive protocols in reporting black-on-white misbehavior, while inflating the flimsiest allegations of white-on-black misbehavior to the level of national crises.

We gut admissions exams for police and firefighter jobs so that blacks can be hired, and pay extravagant compensation to applicants who failed the un-gutted exams. We likewise gut standards for college debate, replacing structured, reasoned argument with incoherent squawking.

We have pretty much dismantled our civilization in an effort to accommodate blacks.

And still they complain.

The Ta-Nehisi Coateses, Eric Holders, and Maya Angelous seem, in their impenetrable narcissism, to hear their own voices as the groans of an oppressed race from under the iron heel of White Supremacy.

Those voices sound to me more like the whining of pampered pets.[91]

We decided to try and make, in the wishes of Jet writer Simeon Booker, the world "a better place to live," by investing untold trillions—and lowering standards universally—to uplift Black people.

The result?

Our civilization was dismantled.

Even if you think Apollo 11 and the subsequent Moon missions were only about "collecting moon rocks," it should be quite obvious now such a rock is worth far, far more than a house in 83 percent Black Detroit.

---

[91] Derbyshire, "On Maya Angelou."

29

The Pioneer Plaque is Racist: How *Ebony's* 1969 Editorial on the Moon Landing Outlined the Future

December 10th, 2012

For some reason, I was intrigued by what *Ebony* magazine published in the months after the successful Apollo 11 mission to the Moon. Well, the September 1969 issue of *Ebony* didn't disappoint, proudly boasting this editorial:

When on July 20th at 10:56 p.m. EDT, Astronaut Neil A. Armstrong first set foot that new world, the moon, he spoke carefully, as if to be sure not to slur a single syllable, words which he knew would go down in history. "That's one small step for man, he said and, after a slight pause, "One giant leap for mankind." Armstrong and his fellow Astronaut Edwin E. Aldrin Jr. walked on the surface of the moon. They proved that space suits would withstand the 250-degree heat of the lunar sun and that man could adjust to walking in the lesser gravity of the moon's atmosphere. They proved that travel and living on other planets is within human accomplishment as they explored the "front porch" of outer space and planted the American flag in lunar soil. They proved that man's space science frontiers are almost limitless and that it is now only a matter of time before man can journey to Mars, to Venus and beyond. Armstrong and Aldrin, like Columbus, opened doors to wider horizons for man. But is man ready for wider horizons?
Can We Learn From the Past?

When Columbus made his voyage of discovery with his flotilla of three tiny ships, he was sailing into waters far more unchartered than the space traveled by Armstrong, Aldrin and Astronaut Michael Collins, pilot of the mother ship Columbia while the lunar module Eagle descended to the moon's surface. In a world which most considered flat, Columbus argued that the earth was really round and that one could get to China by sailing west. He was not able to send unmanned vehicles ahead of him to bring back data. Once his ships had gone beyond the sight of land, Columbus had no means of communicating with those on shore. He was alone on a seemingly endless sea which most of his men believed ended with a dropoff into endless space at the edge of the world.

That Columbus could continue attests to this strong faith in the theories of a few scientists of his day who believed along with that the earth was round. Today, the faith in the men of science is so great that few people ever question sciences eventual ability to solve a problem—the only question is, how soon can it be done?

The Doors Columbus Opened

The daring Columbus opened doors to his world just as great for his time as the moon walkers did for ours. And, like the people of Columbus' time, we may well not be ready for such progress. Columbus, unknowingly, gave to the rulers of Europe two huge and fantastically rich continents— North and South America. Columbus took the one small step for man but what about the "one giant leap for mankind?" What did the rulers do with his gift? The explorers of the new world were soon followed by the exploiters. Britain, Spain, and France, ignoring the "savages" who inhabited the lands across the sea, laid claim to every piece they could and eventually fought each other over it. The Europeans brought plague, measles, small pox, and venereal diseases to the natives and took back gold, silver and, eventually, rum, sugar, cotton, and potatoes.

White Christians despoiled Aztec and Mayan temples and carried precious religious artifacts back to Europe to grace the courts of kings and queens or to be melted down into gold and silver ingots. The men who followed the ex-plorers were heartless conquistadores seeking on fortunes of war—and their wars were primarily against almost de-fenseless natives.

But What of the Settlers?

But what of the settlers who followed the explorers and exploiters? Didn't they develop the land bring law and order to the wilderness? Actually, Columbus' discovery of America eventually lead to one of the most infamous and long-lasting rapes of all history. Settlers in the Americas found that most profitable crops were sugar cane, cotton and tobacco and that they all required tremendous manpower. To fill this need, there developed in both North and South America a system of slavery of black people unmatched in the history of man. Literally millions of black people, men, women and children, were captured in Africa and transported like cattle to till the fields and harvest the crops in the Americas. If the machine age had not come along, it is entirely possible that black men would still be in actual slavery to this day.

What About Today?

Man today is at the threshold of traveling throughout space, of visiting unknown star and perhaps eventually making contact with intelligent beings on other planets. But is earthman ready for this? The answer just has to be "No."

Astronaut Armstrong took "one small step for man" when he planted his left foot in the dust of the moon for the first time. But his "giant leap for mankind" is still in the future. As space scientists continue to explore the universe, what do they plan to say to any intelligent being they might find on Mars or Venus or any of the millions of other stars and planets in this universe?

Are they going to say, "We are from planet Earth. We have millions of people starving to death back home so we thought we'd drop by to see how you are faring." Are they going to admit that the people of a nation such as the United States cannot get along because some are black and some are white?

Are they going to tell others that on Earth nations spend more on armaments and war than they do for housing, education, culture, and perhaps food? Are they ready to admit to Martians, Venusians or what have you that Earthmen lock their doors and bar their windows to keep fellow Earthmen from stealing their possessions? Will they admit that Earthmen who can send men to the moon cannot solve the problems of human transportation on earth? Are they going to tell of dishonest politicians, thieving city officials, bribed judges, incompetent teachers and ambitious citizens who will sell their birthrights for a mess of pottage?

Let's Wait Awhile

There are many who object to the space program because they feel that the money could be better spent finding solutions to the problems mentioned above. But the money does not matter that much. Mankind today has proved that it can do just about whatever it wants to do. It can bring equality to all men in "one giant leap" it really wants to. It can solve the problem of world hunger. It can eliminate war. But mankind won't do any of these things and so, perhaps we should forget about trying to contact intelligent beings in outer space. After all, what can we say to them?[92]

Am I wrong in stating that the editorial advice from *Ebony* magazine became the official policy of the United States government? Colleges and universities in America teach the exact same version of history that *Ebony* established in "Giant Leap for Mankind," engaging in an ever-increasing orgy of anti-White rhetoric in the halls of higher education.

To think: just three years after this editorial appeared, Carl Sagan was somehow able to slip the "Pioneer Plaque" on board the Pioneer 10 and Pioneer 11 spacecraft. Perhaps the most racist example of White supremacy imaginable, the "Pioneer Plaque" is a pictorial message for extraterrestrials with several geometric symbols that would help an advanced civilization

---

[92] Jet Magazine, "Giant Leap for Mankind."

deduce the origins of the spacecraft. On the plaque is the image of naked White man and a White female, an unsettling reminder to the writers of *Ebony* of the true source of the genius behind the missions to space.

I first read about the "Pioneer Plaque" in a copy of Carl Sagan's "Cosmos" some years ago; now, I find myself smiling at the thought that someday an advanced alien civilization might retrieve either the Pioneer 10 and Pioneer 11 spacecraft, decode the message, and send emissaries to make contact with what *Ebony* dubbed "earthmen".

Of course, when the Pioneer 10 and Pioneer 11 spacecrafts were launched, Atlanta, Birmingham, Detroit, Memphis, Newark, Rochester, Baltimore, and even Camden were still cities; California was actually an American state; and the future for NASA appeared to be Mars, instead of outreach to Muslims.[93]

Were these alien emissaries, summoned to earth by a peaceful message aboard the Pioneer 10 or Pioneer 11, to appear in 2012 America, they'd find a civilization mysteriously under the directive of an unsigned editorial from *Ebony* magazine.

Published back in September of 1969.

We could have been on Mars, but we had to fund Black-Run America.

---

[93] Moskowitz, "NASA chief says."

30

Magnificent Desolation: The Apollo Rocket Versus the Mule Cart (A Precursor to the Water Bill Protests in 83% Black Detroit)

July 20th, 2014

It's fitting that as the 45th anniversary of the initial Moon landing, the successful Apollo 11 mission culminating on July 20th, 1969 with Buzz Aldrin and Neal Armstrong walking on the Moon, the 83 percent Black city of Detroit sees protests over unpaid water bills:

Detroit's crackdown on delinquent water customers bubbled over with a public protest Friday following concerns voiced by a federal judge overseeing the city's historic bankruptcy case.

Hundreds of people descended upon downtown Hart Plaza, with many migrating from a conference for progressive Democrats at the nearby Cobo Conference Center.

"We need more water, not less water," said Democratic U.S. Rep. John Conyers, addressing the crowd through a bullhorn on a makeshift stage around the plaza's obelisk-like art installation.

Opposition has been building in Detroit for months after officials at the city's Water and Sewerage Department in March said they would shut off water service to delinquent customers. Critics, including a United Nations panel, have said that water is a basic human right, especially in the nation's largest city to file for bankruptcy protection, one year ago.

Even so, U.S. Bankruptcy Judge Steven Rhodes said this week in court that the water issue was generating bad publicity for the city and told the department to offer more repayment options.[94]

"The Water issue was generating bad publicity for the city," said Judge Rhodes.

Well then, tell the citizens of the 83 percent Black city to pay their water bill, or else suffer the same fate as those non-Black citizens across the country who refuse to pay their water utility bill: have it turned off.

Never forget, what *Instauration* magazine dubbed "one of the sorrier moments in the saga of mankind" was Reverend Abernathy leading a mule caravan to Cape Canaveral before the first manned Moon landing. The money, he whined, should go to the poor and not be thrown away on space.[95]

In another edition of the magazine, a writer penned these words:

Reporters wrote that it was "legitimate" for Rev. Ralph Abernathy, who is often treated as some kind of Negro deity, to take poor families and a symbolic mule team to Cape Kennedy to protest against the moon flight and its vast expenditure when so many earthlings live in poverty and squalor. With whites upon the threshold of the most fabulous voyage of exploration of all time, Negro poverty and white selfishness were the liberal-minority coalition's overriding consideration. The obscuring triviality of this obsessional view of the moon flight was and is truly astounding. Like all fixation or emotional arrests of the personality, it is a form of insanity—in this instance a mouse-like insanity, deliberately depreciating Nordic heroism and achievement. Once the insanity is properly implanted, it follows logically that if

---

[94] Dolan, "Detroit's Water Cutoffs."
[95] Instauration, "Faustian Lapse."

Ralph Abernathy's protest, which in reality was nothing more than a protest against the white man's incomparable superiority, was "legitimate," the space flights themselves were and are "illegitimate."[96]

Reverend Ralph Abernathy, the man who succeeded Martin Luther King as the chief agitator for Blackness, was lauded in the pages of *Jet* magazine for his mule-cart procession (it should be noted this march against Apollo by Blacks set the stage for the water bills protest we currently see in 83 percent Black Detroit, and the mindset that marching will bend White civilization to accept any Black demand).

Simeon Booker would write:

Rev. Ralph Abernathy, the leader many predicted couldn't fill the shoes of Dr. Martin Luther King Jr., became a giant for millions of Americans at Cape Kennedy. No project he has devised reached more people and served a role as his attendance at the launching of Apollo 11.

There wasn't much enthusiasm among American blacks to follow the moon flight. Even though NASA spent billions in one of its precise managerial operations, its directors disregarded equal opportunity programs. NASA has one of the poorest minority hiring among U.S. agencies.

While following the activity at Cape Kennedy, a TV viewer sees very few—if any—black engineers, scientists, or computer programmers. On top of this, the vast outlay of money ($24 billion) to put a man on the moon emptied the U.S. treasury of fund for worthwhile earthly projects—like housing, welfare, schools and jobs.

But Rev. Ralph Abernathy followed the example of his leader, Dr. King, to keep the faith. He refused to see millions of black boys and girls "give up" on the American Dream. He had to get to Cape Kennedy. He had to call the Cape "Holy Ground." He had to conclude: "The ground will be even more holy when we feed the poor."

---

[96] Instauration, "NASA: The Rocket versus the Mule."

He and his followers bunched together, sang *We Shall Overcome*—some day. They trooped from the Cape, as the only major Negro participants in the launching.

One highlight of the Cape launching was the confrontation of Abernathy and NASA's Thomas Paine. The meeting took place in an open field just inside the center's front gate. Abernathy, leading two mules humorously named Jim Eastland and George Wallace, was followed by hundreds of poor carrying picket signs. Paine listened to Abernathy's eloquent plea for the poor. Said Abernathy: "I'm profoundly moved by our nation's scientific achievements in space, and by the heroism of the three astronauts." Calling the moonshot "one of man's noblest ventures," Abernathy said: "But I have not come to Cape Kennedy merely to experience the thrill of this historic launching. I am here to demonstrate with poor people in a symbolic way against the tragic and inexcusable gulf that exists between America's technological abilities and our social injustices."

Paine agreed with the poor people's goals.[97]

That NASA didn't implement Equal Opportunity Commission Goals (EEOC) goals as a priority ahead of landing men on the Moon is the primary reason Apollo 11, 12, 14, 15, 16, and 17 saw twelve White men successfully walk on the Moon, courtesy of the ingenious contributions of individual White people back home on earth.

Ebony magazine would publish an equally polemic, racial denunciation of the Apollo program:

Few efforts outside of war have caused such a sustained flexing of America's scientific, technological and industrial muscle as has the race to the moon. Since the late President John F. Kennedy promised in 1961 that an American would walk on the lunar surface before 1970, the nation has spent more than $24 billion and funneled the work of small armies

97 Jet Magazine, "Blacks Scarce as Men."

of scientists, engineers, technicians, production workers and laborers toward Cape Kennedy.

To many people, the purpose of the moon program—as well as its planning and execution—have seemed as remote as the astronaut's destination. Especially to the nation's black poor, watching on unpaid-for television sets in shacks and slums, the countdowns, the blastoffs, the orbiting and landings had the other-worldly aliens—though not the drama—of a science fiction movie. From Harlem to Watts, the first moon landing in July of last year was viewed cynically as one small step for "The Man," and probably a giant leap in the wrong direction for mankind. Large segments of the rest of the population, except perhaps at the time of the first landing, were merely bored.[98]

No Blacks, in the eyes of *Ebony* writers, meant the landing was "boring" or illegitimate.

But the lack of implementing an agenda of affirmative action and EEOC-mandated hires or promotions would catch up with NASA:

For the second time this month, a Senate committee expressed doubts about the sincerity of a NASA promise to improve its record of hiring minorities and women.

Sen. Frank Moss (D. Utah) said yesterday, after a three-hour hearing before his Aeronautical and Space Sciences Committee that he intends to bring NASA back perhaps every three months to see how rapidly its record improves.

NASA does not dispute claims that its minority employment, 5.6 percent as of last May . . . is the lowest of all government agencies.

But after the agency outlined its Equal Employment Opportunity goals for 1974, several senators indicated they didn't think the goals justified NASA's statement that it was "deeply committed" to "equal opportunity."

---

[98] Ebony, "How Blacks View Mankind's."

"I don't quite feel a sense of urgency," said Sen. Howard Metzenbaum (D. Ohio)." . . . I feel they're modest goals, and they haven't yet been worked down to the lower levels . . ."

[George Lowe, NASA deputy administrator] replied that EEO was at the top of NASA's rarity list, but could not be accomplished "overnight."

"What's even more disconcerting is to see NASA groping for sympathy with a continuing flow apologies and explana-tions," said Sen. James Abourezk (D. ·S.D.).

On Jan. 11, Sen. William Proxmire (D. ·Wis.) ordered NASA to report quarterly on its EEO progress to his Senate Appropriations Subcommittee, which oversees NASA's budged. He cited ". . . NASA's extremely poor record in en-forcing its equal employment opportunity program."[99]

You can land on the Moon, explore other worlds and embark on the greatest journey in man's history, or dedicate every re-source available to advancing the cause of Blackness, thereby retarding all of the Apollo program's successes.

The stars or Detroit.

But this would change, with the desire to travel the road to infinity derailed by a national mandate to take the road to De-troit:

> Today NASA has bowed to pervasive minority racism. The announced Space Shuttle crews are largely a human zoo of minority groups in just the right percentages of each.
>
> It is true the billions of dollars on Apollo could have been spent on the "cities" as the liberals and minorities wanted, but there would have been no moon landing, no spinoff tech-nology, no glorious achievement to remind us of who we are and what we can be. Just more blacks.
>
> After several Apollo flights, interest in space flagged. NASA proposals for regular moon flights, a lunar base, and a manned expedition to Mars in the 1980s were turned down. NASA became a holding operation, concentrating on

---

[99] Scott, "Senators Eye NASA EEO Goals."

unmanned missions such as the Viking landing on Mars and the flybys of Jupiter and Saturn. Engineers and scientists were laid off in the aerospace industry by the droves. Even Wernher Von Braun retired from NASA in 1972.[100]

"Just more blacks" is what we got, with the residents of 83 percent black Detroit believing paying a water bill is now beneath them, with free water a human right:

> In the 50 years since the onset of the "Great Society," the United States has spent nearly $22 trillion and implemented 80 welfare programs with the goal of reducing poverty. How has it worked? Not well, writes Edwin Feulner, founder of the Heritage Foundation. Material poverty has fallen over the last half-century, says Feulner. Today, the average poor household has food on the table, not to mention air-conditioning, cable television and Internet access. However, he explains that the War on Poverty also created negative incentives:
> • Welfare gave single mothers larger payments than married mothers, encouraging women not to marry the fathers of their children.
> • Children who grew up without both parents in their households began to see single-parenthood as normal.[101]

We went to the Moon for $24 billion; we breed an army of individuals who collectively believe paying for water is beneath them for $22 trillion.

I'd like to know the final thoughts of Wernher Von Braun as he left his NASA office for the last time in 1972, the NASA he knew and helped build—whose mandate once was navigating man to the heavens—replaced with the goal of safely navigating Black people and other minority groups into the employ of the "space" administration.

---

[100] Instauration, "The Road To Infinity."
[101] NCPA, "The Consequences of the 'Great Society.'"

Did he see the future he'd never live in reflected in the piti-
ful memory of the Poor People's Campaign demands from July
16th, 1969, at Cape Kennedy, when a mule cart stood next to
his Apollo 11 spacecraft (with the Saturn V rocket system prepared to blast it into the heavens)?

Could he have known then the future wouldn't be the building of a base on the Moon, the start of man's colonization of
solar system, but the colonization of formerly first world cities
by a Black population incapable of sustaining the first world
civilization Whites left behind (see Detroit, Baltimore, Newark,
Gary, Camden, Rochester, Birmingham, Memphis)?

Could he have known that on July 20th, 2014, forty-five
years after the initial Moon landing, Black people ($22 trillion
later) would be protesting their right to be exempted from paying water bills in the former Arsenal of Democracy?

We have completely dismantled our civilization to uplift
Black people (while hordes of brown people scramble across our
borders at the behest of the federal government), and they still
don't think that's enough.

31

Apollo's Efforts Grounded: When NASA Turned to
Star Trek's Lt. Uhura to Recruit the Next
Generation of Non-White Astronauts

July 19th, 2014

The original NASA culture was also imbued with a certain degree of idealism. Professionalism in its classic form requires the bearer to perform a public service, whether it be a doctor curing the sick or an engineer speaking the truth. Two forms of idealism contributed to the NASA culture of the first generation. One was the notion of the space race as the "good war"; the other was the romance of flight.

The airplane was barely twenty-five years old when the first generation of NASA employees was born. Most people traveled by bus or train, if they traveled at all. Flying in airplanes above the ground had a romantic quality that touched many NASA engineers while they were young.

– Howard E. McCurdy, *High Technology*, 83

NASA, along with the companies that performed contract work during Apollo, was a reflection of society's workforce in the late 1960s—mostly white, mostly male.

– Billy Hopkins, *Apollo Moon Missions*, 79

*Civil Rights advocates have been fond for years of pointing out
the incongruity of a nation's being able to send men to the moon
and bring them safely back again without being able to deal
very effectively with its racial problems here on earth. . . .*

    *NASA has compiled a dismal record with respect to female
and minority employment. By now NASA should have learned
that institutionalized sexism and racism give way to neither
simple pieties nor eloquent declarations of principle. Achieving
equitable employment opportunities for women and minorities
in large American institutions requires skill, determination
and sustained effort, just as a successful space program does.
That is a lesson for the 1970s that all major American institutions must learn if the tragedies of the 1960s are to be avoided
in this country's future.*

        – "Racism, Sexism, and Space Ventures," *Washington Post*

*By the time Apollo 11 astronauts had landed on the Moon in
1969, a growing community of dissent had emerged, for whom
America's space success belied a space agency barely integrated by race and gender, even by 1960s standards. Particularly problematic for NASA in the early 1970s was the continued gender and racial exclusivity of its astronaut ranks: the
Moon Race had been one, but NASA would still fly only white
male pilots. Without the Moon Race to shield it, the ethnic and
gender homogeneity of NASA's astronaut corps also suggested
a dissonance between the goals of Apollo (its obsession with
putting "Whitey on the Moon") and the needs of a nation increasingly inclined to view persistent social discrimination as
the leading national concern. Even Star Trek's USS Enterprise
had enjoyed a crew integrated by gender and ethnicity. . . .*

    – Matthew H. Hersch, *Inventing the American Astronaut*, 123

Two White men successfully walked on a different world, forty-five years ago tomorrow. Apollo 11 got them there.

Apollo 12, 14, 15, 16, and 17 would also successfully land on the Moon.

Apollo 18 and 19 would be cancelled, too expensive in an age dominated by the urge for equality and an unprecedented allocation of resources to ensure it happened.

And though the crew of the fictional *Star Trek* was integrated, the NASA that put twelve men on the Moon from 1969–1972 was almost entirely White.

Much to the chagrin of one of the fictional "astronauts" who spent years on the set of the USS Enterprise: the black actress Nichelle Nichols, who played the part of Lt. Uhura on *Star Trek*.

In the pages of *Forbes*, she would be quoted as saying her efforts were successful, because she, "improved NASA's human mission with her single-handed effort to include more women and African-Americans in the space agency of the late 1970s that was dominated by White-male employees."

Nichols would give a speech in 1977, titled "New Opportunities for the Humanization of Space," where she voiced her concerns and the criticisms that been leveled against the space program by the women and minorities whom she had met during her travels.

She would meet with NASA's Associate Administrator for Space Flight, John Yardley, and the Black NASA Assistant Administrator for Equal Opportunity Programs, Dr. Harriet Jenkins, to discuss her speech and why so few minorities were applying to be astronauts:

[S]he talked herself into becoming a recruitment contractor of minorities for NASA's Astronaut Corp. However, she informed those present that in accepting the assignment (contract) her credibility was at stake, and if she found suitably qualified women and minorities for the astronaut program who would subsequently not be selected, then she would "personally file a class-action suit against NASA." She was not going to be used to attract publicity and then have NASA say later that despite all its efforts it could find no qualified women or minorities. NASA concurred.[102]

So, NASA was no longer an organization where merit was the necessary condition for employment or advancement; nothing more than a lack of certain genitalia or an abundance of melanin that would instantly qualify you for NASA employment, and result in your being pushed to the front of astronaut training—or else Lt. Uhura would file a class-action lawsuit.

And people still believe we didn't go to the Moon, when an actress from a fictional show about a future racial Utopia would dictate to NASA just who could be an astronaut.

In an interview with *Smithsonian Magazine*, she'd elaborate her angst with NASA selecting just another "all-white male astronaut corps":

Q: How did you become affiliated with NASA and in what capacity?

A: Ten years after "Star Trek" was cancelled, almost to the day, I was invited to join the board of directors of the newly formed National Space Society. They flew me to Washington and I gave a speech called "New Opportunities for the Humanization of Space" or "Space, What's in it for me?" In [the speech], I'm going where no man or woman dares go. I took NASA on for not including women and I gave some history of the powerful women who had applied and, after five times applying, felt disenfranchised and backed off. [At that time] NASA was having their fifth or sixth recruitment and women and ethnic people [were] staying away in droves. I was asked to come to headquarters the next day and they wanted me to assist them in persuading women and people of ethnic backgrounds that NASA was serious [about recruiting them]. And I said you've got to be

---

[102] Shyler, *Women in Space*, 153.

joking; I didn't take them seriously . . . John Yardley, who I knew from working on a previous project, was in the room and said 'Nichelle, we are serious.' I said OK. I will do this and I will bring you the most qualified people on the planet, as qualified as anyone you've ever had and I will bring them in droves. And if you do not pick a person of color, if you do not pick a woman, if it's the same old, same old, all-white male astronaut corps, that you've done for the last five years, and I'm just another dupe, I will be your worst nightmare.

Q: And what happened?

A: They picked five women, they picked three African-American men, they picked an Asian and the space program has represented all of us ever since. That is my contribution and that is one of the things I am most proud of.[103]

It should be noted that in 1976, NASA's Astronaut Selection Board had set new guidelines on how to recruit future astronauts. This was before a fictional lieutenant from a television would threaten a lawsuit if Black and women candidates weren't selected:

Phase I
    A. NASA determines final qualification requirements.
    B. Prepare recruiting information packets, which will include:
        1. Description of Space Shuttle program.
        2. Qualification requirements.
            a. Pilots.
            b. Mission specialists.
        3. Description of selection process.
        4. Application blank(s).
    C. Meet with special interest groups, such as National Organization for Women, NAACP, and the League of United Latin American Citizens.
        1. Explain qualification criteria rationale.

---

[103] Childs, "How Nichelle Nichols Launched."

    2. Enlist aid in publicizing recruitment effort and
      identification of candidates.
    3. Provide information packets for distribution.
  D. Prepare press kits.
Phase II
  A. Announce recruitment program to the public.
    1. Possible press conference; consider participation
      by special interest group representatives.
    2. Distribute press kit.
    3. Provide all NASA public speakers with
      information kit for use in every public
      appearance.
    4. Place recruitment advertisements in appropriate
      publications.[104]

During the 1960s and the buildup to the Apollo program, not one special interest had a say in anything NASA did.

We landed on the Moon with Apollo 11, 12, 14, 15, 16 and 17 then.

The post-1972 NASA gave us meetings with the NAACP, to dictate how NASA would select pilots for space travel.

NASA would then film a commercial with Lt. Uhura herself, Nichelle Nichols, dressed in blue overalls of an astronaut, delivering a recruitment pitch on national television. She read from a teleprompter:

Oh, Hi. I'm Nichelle Nichols. It kind of looks like when I was Lieutenant Uhura on the starship Enterprise, doesn't it. Well, now there's a twentieth century Enterprise, an actual space vehicle built by NASA and designed to put us in the business of space—not merely space exploration. NASA's Enterprise is a space shuttlecraft, built to make regularly scheduled runs into space and back. Now, the shuttle will be taking scientists and engineers, men and women of all races, into space—just like the astronauts crew on the starship

---

[104] Atkinson, *Real Stuff,* 145–6.

Enterprise. That is why I'm speaking to the whole family of humankind—minorities and women included. If you qualify and would like to be an astronaut, *now* is the time! This *your* NASA![105]

After 1972, NASA became nothing more than glorified United States Postal Service, dedicated to the same principles that have guided the NAACP since its founding: advancing the interests of non-White people while subverting the interests of Whites.

We went to the Moon.

July 20th, 2014 should be a date we celebrate our genesis into the exploration of new celestial worlds; instead, it's just another date where we see those stars going increasingly out of focus, clouded with the uncertainty of a future where the advancement of minority interests has completely subverted our civilization.

So, congrats Nichelle Nichols: you've ensured the future—for now—is nothing (thankfully) like the liberal world of *Star Trek*; instead, it looks like something out of 1968's *Planet of the Apes*.

Post-1972 NASA is nothing more than a social experiment; knowing we must hitch a ride with the Russians to even get to space in 2014 should be sufficient information in showing how this experiment ended.

Space isn't the final frontier.

Race realism is the final frontier, and acceptance of this truth the way back to the stars.

If not, all roads point to Detroit.

---

[105] Ibid., 63–4.

32

The Meek Shall Inherit the Earth
(Courtesy of your Tax Dollars)

January 12th, 2013

Checkmate, White America.

Right?

You are now dethroned from power, scurrying like rats for the few morsels of hope tossed down by the Managerial Elite of Black-Run America, all the while paying for your own dispossession via a transfer of wealth through taxation.

We could have been on Mars, but instead we paid for Ralph Abernathy's dream of ending poverty, racism, and hunger.

Alleviating hunger via SNAP/EBT cards. When they stop working, we already know what happens.

To pay for this dispossession, NASA and improvements in the transportation infrastructure were abandoned; the goal was to turn all of America into nothing more than Newark and Detroit:

New research from the Republicans on the Senate Budget Committee shows that over the last 5 years, the U.S. has spent about $3.7 trillion on welfare. Here's a chart, showing that spending versus transportation, education, and NASA spending:

"We have just concluded the 5th fiscal year since President Obama took office. During those five years, the federal government has spent a total $3.7 trillion on approximately 80 different means-tested poverty and welfare programs.

The common feature of means-tested assistance programs is that they are graduated based on a person's income and, in contrast to programs like Social Security or Medicare, they are a free benefit and not paid into by the recipient," says the minority side of the Senate Budget Committee.

"The enormous sum spent on means-tested assistance is nearly five times greater than the combined amount spent on NASA, education, and all federal transportation projects over that time. ($3.7 trillion is not even the entire amount spent on federal poverty support, as states contribute more than $200 billion each year to this federal nexus—primarily in the form of free low-income health care.)[106]

What type of world will $3.7 trillion help fund? How about one where two children left home alone when a house fire broke out being of least concern to the aunt involved (who left them home alone), compared to the status of her EBT/SNAP food stamp card:

MEMPHIS, Tenn.—Screams filled the evening sky as family members try to cope with what happened Monday in a South Memphis community. Two children, 2-year-old Catareon Dunn and 3-year old Ladareon Dunn, were left home alone shortly before a fire broke out.

Officials responded to a house fire call at 1236 Effie Road off Mt. Moriah. The two boys were left unattended while their mother and aunt left the house to go drop off a friend. Sometime after that, 911 received a call from neighbors saying the house was on fire.

Neighbors say they heard screams coming from the house and rushed to the back door to try and rescue the children. However, when they got there, the flames and smoke were too powerful for them to enter.

When the children were finally pulled from the house, onlookers described them as looking like "rag dolls." Both were rushed to the Le Bonheur Children's Hospital in

---

[106] Halper, "Report: US Spent $3.7 Trillion."

critical condition. Ladareon died shortly thereafter. Catare-on remains in critical condition.

The children's aunt, Marilyn Wilson, who left the house with the mother, said she had no regrets about leaving the children home alone, "No, I really don't because if they had been there by themselves, I don't know if the boys set the house on fire or somebody threw something in there to set it on fire. I really need to get in there to see if my purse burned up. I had my Food Stamp Card and everything in there."

The cause of the fire is under investigation by the Memphis Fire Department.[107]

A food stamp card can be replaced. Children cannot.

Worse, once a city loses its founding population, expecting to maintain the same standard-of-living with a new demographic in political power means you get Memphis 2013.

But what happens when those seeking handouts overwhelm a city? What happens when a city no longer has enough White producers to fleece, to help pay for the cradle-to-grave lifestyle of those dispossessing them?

The welfare office tells them to go elsewhere, seeking new White towns to conquer.

Like locusts, breeding in one location and bleeding all natural resources there dry, they spread in search of a new land to overwhelm:

Cheryl Johns found it curious that poor people from Newark were calling Altoona, a small rural town 260 miles away in the hills of Central Pennsylvania, looking for places to live.

Johns, who runs the Altoona Housing Authority, first noticed the trend a few years ago, when her office started getting requests from Newarkers to fill out applications for government-subsidized apartments.

Then the odd trickle became a deluge.

---

[107] Hunter, "House Fire Leaves 1 Dead."

Now Altoona is accusing Newark of referring clients to them, and a Pennsylvania congressman has asked New Jersey Gov. Jon Corzine to intervene.

"What I'd like to see stopped is this flood of people coming from New Jersey on a daily basis," Johns said yesterday. "I'm not denying a housing application to anyone. But the housing problem in Newark needs to be fixed. Don't push your problem to Altoona."

The spat apparently stems from the severe shortage of affordable housing in Newark and other parts of New Jersey, where home costs are among the top in the nation and federal subsidies are shrinking. That, New Jersey officials say, has made people desperate.

The problem is particularly acute in Newark, where 28 percent of the 273,546 residents live in poverty. The city housing authority, wracked by layoffs and fiscal mismanagement, is now bracing for massive funding cuts and has closed a waiting list for subsidized apartments.

Demand for affordable housing also outstrips supply in Altoona, a city of 49,523 people, 18 percent of whom live in poverty. Johns said many applicants have to wait a couple years for public housing units and so-called Section 8 rental vouchers.

Since the calls started, the Altoona Housing Authority has placed about eight families from Newark in its apartments, and given Section 8 vouchers to another six, Johns said. Other Newarkers have found cheap apartments from private landlords in Altoona, she said.

Those numbers aren't a problem, she said. But she started getting upset a few months ago, when requests for applications from Newarkers began pouring into her office. Anywhere from three to five calls were coming in every day—twice the previous rate. When her employees asked why Altoona, the callers gave one of two answers: a friend told them about Altoona, or they got the number off a flier in Newark. Many of them cited crime and poor conditions in Newark's public housing complexes.

That set Johns off. With help from a local state senator, she got a hold of the offending flier, purportedly taken from a Newark welfare office, which listed the numbers of the Altoona Housing Authority and a private complex in Williamsport, Pa. (where officials say there haven't been any complaints).

Robin Moore, 37, saw the flier during a January 2006 visit to her caseworker in the Essex County welfare offices on Rector Street in Newark. She loved her hometown, and she'd never even heard of Altoona. But she was tired of working 50-hour weeks as a customer service representative just to pay the bills on the two-bedroom apartment on Osborne Terrace she shared with her husband, three children and grandson. And she worried about the drugs and crime.

So she called the number and got an application for an Altoona Housing Authority apartment. Her first trip to Altoona, to fill out more paperwork, was a 15-hour Greyhound bus ride. In March, she got approved to move her family into a tidy four-bedroom apartment in Fairview Hills for less rent than she paid for the smaller place in Newark. She's collecting unemployment insurance and her husband works as a housing authority groundskeeper.

But Pennsylvania officials weren't satisfied.

In a May 21 column in the Altoona Mirror newspaper, Mayor Wayne Hippo alleged that "more than a few" of the New Jersey migrants "have been involved in the drug and crime trade." He didn't mention Newark by name.

"Personally, I'm sickened that somebody in a New Jersey welfare office decided to 'solve' some of New Jersey's problems by creating a list of Pennsylvania cities to send their troubled cases to," Hippo wrote.

On Wednesday, Johns fired an angry letter off to Keith Kinard, director of the Newark Housing Authority, accusing his staff of referring their clients to Altoona. [108]

---

[108] Schuppe, "Newarkers take Altoona express."

In some alternate America, the riots in Detroit and Newark of the late 1960s were greeted with volley after volley of bullets, fired by members of the National Guard. The Kerner Commission was never assembled, for the blame on the disturbances/insurrection/rebellion was placed squarely in the direction of the Black community.

Those cities didn't become incubators for every negative social characteristic associated with the Black underclass, the type of pathologies breeding dysfunction never before seen on Earth.

Ralph Abernathy wasn't allowed to protest the Apollo launch in Florida, for he and his ilk never came close to Cape Canaveral on their horse and buggy.

In that alternate America, the money spent over the past forty years on welfare, social engineering (Head Start, Housing and Urban Development programs, diversity initiatives, etc.), went to the building of a permanent base on the Moon, from which a space port was constructed that served as the launching pad for colonizing the stars.

And for the launch of the ship that would put man on Mars.

Instead, a city like Wilkes-Barre, Pennsylvania gets to taste the type of community Blacks have created in the shadows of skyscrapers found in cities long ago abandoned by White people.[109]

We could have been on Mars, but you had to fund Black-Run America instead.

---

[109] Kersey, "Wilkes-Barre, Pennsylvania."

33

Rev. Abernathy's Dream Comes True: Breaking Down SNAP/EBT Card Usage by Race and County

On November 28th, 2009, *The New York Times* published a map that, were it properly read and studied, would forever end the debate as to whether or not America is still an exceptional nation.[110]

The residue of exceptionalism still exists, though it is being crowded out by massive illegal immigration and completely drowned out in formerly mighty cities now little more than incubators for the next underclass uprising (à la Hurricane Katrina in New Orleans).

The New York Times article carried the title, "Food Stamp Usage Across the Country," and featured an interactive map that allowed the user to see the overall breakdown of people—children, the White percentage of the population, the Black percentage of the population—receiving EBT/Food Stamps by county in America.

The map allows you to look at the country (county-by-county) to see all recipients and changes since 2007.

For those ignorant of statistics, an article accompanying the map spells out the racial breakdown in simple percentages:

Now nearly 12 percent of Americans receive aid—28 percent of blacks, 15 percent of Latinos and 8 percent of whites.

---

[110] Bloch, et al., "Food Stamp Usage."

Benefits average about $130 a month for each person in the household, but vary with shelter and child care costs.[111]

This data is outdated (with food stamp spending doubling since 2008), though it does provide an invaluable foundation to surmising the racial quicksand the historic American population finds itself knee-deep in currently.

> The financial crisis is over and the recession ended in 2009. But one of the federal government's biggest social welfare programs, which expanded when the economy convulsed, isn't shrinking back alongside the recovery.
>
> Enrollment in the Supplemental Nutrition Assistance Program, as the modern-day food-stamp benefit is known, has soared 70% since 2008 to a record 47.8 million as of December 2012. Congressional budget analysts think participation will rise again this year and dip only slightly in coming years.[112]

Using the data from *The New York Times* map on food stamp usage, we have put together a breakdown of the racial dynamics of EBT/SNAP usage for America's biggest cities; it should be quite obvious that the fear of a contagion spreading—turning large segments of the population into ravenous zombies—isn't what's behind the thinking of preppers, survivalists, and gun enthusiasts.

What makes America exceptional is that so few do so much to keep this system alive, while simultaneously funding population growth in racial groups that do so little to keep the system alive.

Just look at the disparity in places like Portland (Oregon), Seattle, Madison, Milwaukee, Denver, Minneapolis and St. Paul, and you'll understand that George Romero is completely

---

[111] DeParle and Gebeloff, "Food Stamp Use Soars."
[112] Paletta and Porter, "Use of Food Stamps."

wrong when it comes to the disaster scenario that needs to filmed.

And remember, this data lacks the past four years of hyper-growth in EBT/SNAP usage; the reliance on food stamps by people of color (and on the continued system of taxing Whites to pay for this artificial population growth) represents the greatest threat to stability of the system.

The Day the EBT Card Stops is the moment when places like Macon, Memphis, Rockford, and Akron experience tiny outbreaks of madness, much like the initial instances of a zombie outbreak, when hospitals are overwhelmed with strange "bites" and the police are ill-prepared to deal with an insurgency. It's vital you use the data above—realizing the numbers are four years old—and consider the implications of living in counties with sizable EBT/SNAP users.

Study this breakdown of just who relies on EBT/SNAP in major cities. Just remember, these numbers don't represent the past four years of insane growth in reliance on EBT/SNAP benefits, but should give a huge hint as to which group is seeing the greatest growth in benefits.

County	City	Overall Percent	Percent of Whites	Percent of Blacks
Jackson (Missouri)	Kansas City	21%	11%	48%
Sedgwick (Kansas)	Wichita	12%	8%	36%
Boone (Missouri)	Columbia	15%	10%	63%
St. Louis City	St. Louis	36%	10%	60%
Pulaski (Arkansas)	Little Rock	14%	5%	29%
Shelby (TN)	Memphis	25%	6%	42%
Hinds (Miss)	Jackson	23%	5%	31%
Davidson (TN)	Nashville	17%	9%	33%
Knox (TN)	Knoxville	13%	11%	36%

Jefferson (AL)	Birming-ham	13%	4%	27%
Montgomery (AL)	Montgom-ery	20%	3%	32%
Mobile (AL)	Mobile	19%	10%	37%
Leon (FL)	Tallahas-see	10%	4%	23%
Bibb (GA)	Macon	24%	7%	40%
Fulton (GA)	Atlanta	14%	2%	30%
DeKalb (GA)	Atlanta	13%	2%	23%
Chatam (GA)	Savannah	14%	4%	28%
Duval (FL)	Jackson-ville	14%	7%	27%
Charleston (SC)	Charleston	12%	3%	30%
Richland (SC)	Columbia	14%	4%	26%
Mecklenburg (NC)	Charlotte	12%	3%	37%
Guilford (NC)	Greens-boro	13%	5%	26%
Norfolk (VA)	Norfolk	17%	4%	32%
Richmond (VA)	Richmond (VA)	19%	2%	34%
Orange (FL)	Orlando	11%	4%	21%
Miami-Dade (FL)	Miami	17%	3%	25%
(Baltimore)	Baltimore (MD)	24%	8%	32%
New Castle (DE)	Wilming-ton (DE)	10%	4%	24%
Philadelphia (Penn)	Philadel-phia	26%	9%	37%
Camden (NJ)	Camden	9%	3%	20%
Mercer (NJ)	Trenton	6%	2%	17%
Essex (NJ)	Newark	11%	2%	20%

Alleghany	Pittsburgh	11%	6%	38%
Erie (NY)	Buffalo	13%	7%	40%
Monroe (NY)	Rochester	12%	5%	42%
Onondaga (NY)	Syracuse	12%	7%	43%
Albany (NY)	Albany	9%	5%	33%
Cumberland (Maine)	Portland (Maine)	12%	9%	56%
Suffolk (Mass)	Boston	16%	6%	28%
Hamilton (Ohio)	Cincinnati	12%	5%	33%
Montgomery (Oh)	Dayton	14%	9%	36%
Franklin (Ohio)	Columbus	15%	9%	41%
Summit (Ohio)	Akron	13%	8%	40%
Cuyahoga (Ohio)	Cleveland	18%	8%	40%
Lucas (Ohio)	Toledo	19%	12%	46%
Lake (Indiana)	Gary	17%	8%	37%
Marion	Indianapolis	17%	11%	34%
Wayne (Michigan)	Detroit	22%	11%	38%
Genesse (Mich.)	Flint	23%	16%	52%
Kent (Michigan)	Grand Rapids	14%	9%	54%
Cook (Illinois)	Chicago	15%	4%	34%
Winnebago (IL)	Rockford	16%	10%	46%
Dane (WS)	Madison	7%	4%	51%
Milwaukee (WS)	Milwaukee	20%	5%	45%

Brown (WS)	Green Bay	9%	6%	60%
Hennepin (MN)	Minneapolis	9%	2%	47%
Ramsey (MN)	St. Paul	12%	4%	49%
Polk (Iowa)	Des Moines	11%	6%	35%
Linn (Iowa)	Cedar Rapids	10%	6%	39%
Douglas (Neb.)	Omaha	10%	5%	37%
Lancaster (Neb.)	Lincoln	7%	6%	33%
Tulsa (Okla.)	Tulsa	11%	8%	34%
Oklahoma (County)	Okla. City	14%	10%	36%
Caddo Parrish	Shreveport	20%	7%	35%
East Baton Rouge	Baton Rouge	16%	3%	32%
Orleans Parrish	New Orleans	22%	3%	32%
Harris County	Houston	9%	3%	21%
Dallas County	Dallas	11%	4%	25%
Travis	Austin	11%	3%	25%
El Paso (Colorado)	Colorado Springs	8%	8%	22%
Denver County	Denver	10%	9%	52%
Salt Lake County	Salt Lake City	8%	6%	37%
Maricopa	Phoenix	11%	6%	30%
Los Angeles County	Los Angeles	8%	3%	24%
Fresno County	Fresno	18%	10%	43%
San Fran County	San Francisco	4%	2%	24%

Sacramento County	Sacramento	11%	8%	34%
Multnomah	Portland (OR)	17%	11%	47%
King	Seattle	9%	5%	31%
Spokane County	Spokane	16%	14%	33%
San Diego County	San Diego	5%	3%	17%
Washington D.C.		17%	1%	30%
Richmond (GA)	Augusta	23%	10%	35%

34

BET.com Notes Government Shutdown Hurts Black Federal Workers: Why Are So Many Black Public Sector Employees "Non-Essential?"

October 4th, 2013

The government shutdown.

No visits to Ellis Island.

The World War II Memorial.

Sadly, the Liberty Bell is closed too.

But the true victim in the closing of non-essential government personnel (and closing of national parks) isn't the American people.

No sir.

It's the usual suspects:

The telephones in the office of Rep. G.K. Butterfield are ringing off the hook with calls from constituents who've been furloughed due to the federal government shutdown.

"They're saying they want to go back to work; they have obligations to meet," the North Carolina lawmaker told BET.com. "This thing is having a devastating effect on workers all across the country. African-Americans are suffering disproportionately because they're disproportionately represented in the federal government."

African-Americans working in the federal workplace represent to a large extent the Black middle class, said Rep. Charles Rangel (New York). Deeming them non-essential and sending them home during the shutdown could have a detrimental effect on their families and their communities.

The Social Security Administration on Tuesday announced that 16,000 employees in Rep. Elijah Cummings' Baltimore district would be furloughed.

"That's a lot of people," said the Maryland lawmaker. "And across the country, hundreds of thousands of people on furlough don't know whether they're going to be paid for these days."

In past shutdowns, they've been paid retroactively, "but in the climate we're in today, I think there's a 50-50 shot that they'll get paid, which is devastating," Cummings added.

He also worries about the people who depend on the services that African-Americans will have to do without, such as the ability to apply for Medicare, disability and other benefits.

Rep. Karen Bass added to the list the Special Supplemental Nutrition Program for Women, Infants and Children, known as WIC, that is used by low-income African-American and Latino families. More than 8.9 million mothers and children depend on WIC for food vouchers, baby formula and other nutrition needs.

The USDA announced on Oct. 1 that it would suspend the program as a result of the shutdown. States will only be able to continue operating the program for "a week or so" before the money runs out.[113]

The American Experiment has become nothing more than a jobs program for otherwise unemployable Black people, helping create and foster an artificial Black middle class.[114]

Yes, it's an artificial middle class.[115]

---

[113] Jones, "Government Shutdown Hits Blacks."
[114] Williams, "As Public Sector Sheds."
[115] Dade, "Government Job Cuts Threaten."

By the way: did you know that 62 percent those receiving the Special Supplemental Nutrition Program for Women, Infants and Children (WIC) are either Hispanic or Black?

The proportion of Hispanic WIC recipients grew from 35.3 percent in 2000 to 41.9 percent in 2010 while the proportions of black and white WIC recipients have declined from 37.4 to 31.8 per- cent for whites and 21.9 to 20.1 percent for blacks (Conor et al. 2011). This increase in WIC enrollment among Hispanics, relative to whites and blacks, corresponds with a large growth in the Hispanic population from 33.7 million in 2000 to 49.9 million in 2010 (a 47.9 percent increase) and a large increase in the number of Hispanic poor from 7.1 million in 2000 to 13.2 million in 2010 (an 85.1 percent increase) (Dalaker 2001; DeNavas- Walt, Proctor, and Smith 2011).[116]

The National Parks may be closed, but our borders are obviously wide open, so that the next generation of something called an "American" can be imported from Mexico and raised via the racial transfusion of funds from White America (in the form of WIC).

Though White America is essential now for the looting of their hard-earned salaries (eventual retirement funds), in the coming decades, it is these same people who will become increasingly non-essential.

---

[116] Martinez-Schiferl, "WIC Participants."

35

The Walking Deadbeats: What Happens When EBT Cards Stop Working for Good?

October 16th, 2013, VDARE

Last weekend saw the fourth season debut of the popular AMC show *The Walking Dead*, chronicling how a disparate group of Americans survive a zombie apocalypse. The show garnered its highest ratings ever: 16.1 million viewers.

No show could capture the zeitgeist better—because, simultaneously, Americans got a frightening glimpse into a future where government-dependent mobs become the dominant species.

Recipients of the SNAP EBT/Food Stamp card in seventeen states saw their benefits cut off when a simple test of a backup system by Xerox Corp, one of the contractors for the debit-style card, caused a system failure. People trying to make purchases were greeted with a "zero" balance when they tried to check out.[117]

Unfortunately for the collapsing Custodial State, although EBIT was down for less than a day, nature doesn't take days off:

> Shelves in Walmart stores in Springhill and Mansfield, LA were reportedly cleared Saturday night, when the stores allowed purchases on EBT cards even though they were not

---

[117] CBS/AP, "Computer Glitch Blamed."

showing limits. The chaos that followed ultimately required intervention from local police, and left behind numerous carts filled to overflowing, apparently abandoned when the glitch-spurred shopping frenzy ended.

Springhill Police Chief Will Lynd confirms they were called in to help the employees at Walmart because there were so many people clearing off the shelves. He says Walmart was so packed, "It was worse than any black Friday" that he's ever seen.[118]

Note carefully: less than one day of one simple system outage—and chaos erupts that eerily resembles the police looting the Wal-Mart in the days after Hurricane Katrina hit New Orleans. This time local police may not have looted, but it seems not to have occurred to them to *arrest* any of the looters. They say they aren't even going to investigate it unless asked by Wal-Mart.[119]

How can people not have enough food in their homes to cover meals for a mere twenty-four-hour period?

Conservative websites, continuing their pattern of dog-whistling racial angst to generate hits and ad revenue, had a field-day reporting on the Tweets by those adversely effected by the EBT glitch.[120]

Significantly, no-one apparently wants to remember that a similar incident occurred in Clayton County, Georgia in 2011:

Anger and frustration from dozens of Clayton County parents who say their children are going hungry after their food stamps were suddenly cut off.

State officials admit that something went wrong down in Clayton County at the office that administers food stamps and Medicaid but they're still not sure what.

Parents say they can't buy food without those food stamps.

118 Roy, "Walmart shelves in Springhill."
119 McGaughty, "Next step on food."
120 Ryan, "EBT System Goes Down."

Terry Clark says she stood in line for more than six hours at Clayton County's Human Services Office because food stamp help for her six children unexpectedly ended.

"There's no telling my kids we can't eat. I'm not taking no. We don't deserve that. Nobody should go hungry here in Georgia," said Terry Clark.

State officials say the office was overwhelmed Tuesday with dozens of families facing a similar problem. The food stamps are just not there.

"Me and my kids they haven't ate since this morning. I was supposed to get my food stamps yesterday and I got nothing," said a mother.[121]

If you can't care for your children, why have them? Oh wait, that's what Uncle Sam is for.

Today, some 47.6 million Americans—one in six—rely on EBT/SNAP benefits.[122] Back in the good-ole' responsible days of 2008, just 36 million Americans used them. Federal funding for the Supplemental Nutrition Assistance Program (SNAP) program reached $82 billion in 2013, according to Jeff Sessions.[123] Back in 2008 it was just was $39 billion.

Who are these Americans? There does exist a racial breakdown for EBT/SNAP users, though it's somewhat dated.

Now, nearly 12 percent of Americans receive aid: 28 percent of Blacks, 15 percent of Latinos and 8 percent of Whites. Benefits average about $130 a month for each person in the household, but vary with shelter and childcare costs.[124]

At some point in their life, 90 percent of Black children will reportedly be on food stamps—one of the costs imposed the taxpayer by the irresponsible sexual choices of Black males and their female partners (be they White, Black, Asian, or Hispanic—the resultant off-spring is classified as "Black"). See *The New York Times's* interactive map, and my spreadsheet of

[121] Grey, "Clayton Food Stamp Snafu."
[122] Izzo, "Food-Stamp Use Rises."
[123] Ballasy, "Sessions: Food stamp spending."
[124] DeParle and Gebeloff, "Food Stamp Use Soars."

EBT/SNAP card usage by counties based on America's largest cities (broken down by race).

And this doesn't even include the WIC benefit extended to the healthcare of low-income pregnant women. This form of racial socialism extends to the crib, where 62 percent of those receiving WIC benefits are either Hispanic or Black:

> The proportion of Hispanic WIC recipients grew from 35.3 percent in 2000 to 41.9 percent in 2010 while the proportions of black and white WIC recipients have declined from 37.4 to 31.8 per- cent for whites and 21.9 to 20.1 percent for blacks (Conor et al. 2011). [This is misleadingly phrased. It means that about a fifth of WIC recipients are Black, although Blacks are only just over a tenth of the US population. Similarly, Whites under-participate relative to their three-quarters' share of the US population]. This increase in WIC enrollment among Hispanics, relative to whites and blacks, corresponds with a large growth in the Hispanic population from 33.7 million in 2000 to 49.9 million in 2010 (a 47.9 percent increase) and a large increase in the number of Hispanic poor from 7.1 million in 2000 to 13.2 million in 2010 (an 85.1 percent increase).[125]

Hard-working Americans are funding their own demographic displacement.

But there's good news. One company is making a mint administering the EBT-card explosion: JPMorgan Chase & Co.

> "This business is a very important business to JPMorgan," Christopher Paton, managing director of JPMorgan's public-sector payments business, told *Bloomberg News* in 2010. "It's an important business in terms of its size and scale. . . . Right now, volumes have gone through the roof in the past couple of years or so . . . The good news, from JPMorgan's perspective is the infrastructure

---

[125] Martinez-Schiferl, "WIC Participants."

that we built has been able to cope with that increase in volume."[126]

A study released last fall by the Government Accountability Institute (GAI), a government watchdog group, estimated that since 2004 JPMorgan had collected more than $560 million in fees from just eighteen of the states with which it has EBT contracts.[127]

Thus, racial socialism employs corporate welfare to facilitate the demographic tidal wave that could soon overwhelm the historic American nation.

But as we saw when a simple data-processing center went down, the system isn't perfect. And instability, when it occurs, unleashes events no one can predict.

Those 32. 2 million eyeballs glued to *The Walking Dead* on AMC don't have zombies to fear in real life.

What they do have to fear is something infinitely more terrifying: *The Day the EBT Card Runs Out.*

[126] Schweizer, "JP Morgan's Food Stamp Empire."
[127] Ibid.

36

Tick, Tick, Tick

January 29th, 2012

Few have dared confront what will happen on *The Day the EBT Card Runs Out.* This nightmarish scenario is the moment that masters of horror like Clive Barker, Stephen King, Wes Craven, George Romero, Frank Darabont, and other writers and directors avoid, for the implications are far more frighten‐ing than any mere zombie apocalypse, an inextinguishable hockey‐masked killer, or an evil supernatural clown combined.

The Day the EBT Card Runs Out is a real eventuality, one that will play out when the United States federal government can no longer borrow money to dole out entitlements to a grow‐ing population segment that produces nothing. Well, "nothing" is not the best choice of word. It is more accurate to say that the disproportionate amount of crime, requiring quasi‐martial law to be declared in a growing number of cities, forces the funding of the police sector as a notable outgrowth of this de‐mographic.

It is for this reason that Predator drones will take to the sky over cities like Philadelphia, Kansas City, Chicago, St. Louis, Baltimore, Cincinnati, Newark, and Birmingham, all in the name of 'keeping an eye on high crime areas."

So, what happens when those EBT Cards stop working? What happens when the money runs out and they no longer provide the magical ability to provide victuals and provender?

Back in 2009, *The New York Times* produced an interactive map that breaks down EBT card usage by race for every county in America.[128] Please note that Hispanics are lumped in with the "White" category. In 2010, the *NYT* published another map that showed the percentage of growth from 2007 to 2009. The safety net of EBT cards is a growing cost that an absolutely broke federal government will one day be unable to pay.

To understand the disproportionate reliance that Black people have upon the EBT card, take a look at the racial breakdown of Michigan: out of 1,405,515 Blacks in Michigan, 546,135 (39 percent) are on EBT Cards.[129]

A burgeoning Black (no pun intended) market exists in Detroit (84 percent Black), where the EBT card is the de facto currency of the population. Michigan serves as a microcosm for the fraud endemic in the EBT card community:

> Two undercover informants entered Jefferson's Liquor Palace and spotted the owner at the register. "Big baby," said one, "we gon' do this?"
>
> The man behind the counter provided $50 in cash, two bottles of liquor, two porn DVDs and two Viagra pills—all in exchange for taking $280.85 off a food-stamp card, say federal investigators who recorded the deal.
>
> Fraud in the government program that helps the poor has added up to nearly $100 million since 2007, according to the U.S. Agriculture Department. It's a fraction of the more than $40 billion spent to feed people each year, but the crime has become a brazen way for some small stores to literally swipe cash from the U.S. Treasury, especially in the Detroit area.
>
> There have been at least 122 fraud-related convictions of owners or employees in the five-state Midwest region since 2007, nearly double the number from 2004–06, says USDA,

---

[128] DeParle and Gebeloff, "Food Stamp Use Soars."
[129] Wallace, "Black Apocalypse."

which oversees the welfare program. About half of those have occurred in southeastern Michigan.[130]

Remember, these numbers represent 2009 data. A recent survey provided by the Office of Research and Analysis provides a glimpse of the disproportionate reliance that Black people have on the EBT card (remember, Black people comprise only 13 percent of our US population).

Investor's Business Daily has provided a cover story on entitlement usage—sans racial/demographic breakdown—that offers a glimpse of the nightmarish scenario toward which we inch closer to each day:

> If the Republican primaries are any indication, one big debate in the upcoming election will be whether President Obama is pushing the country toward a European-style welfare culture.
>
> Mitt Romney, for example, argues that "over the past three years, Barack Obama has been replacing our merit-based society with an entitlement society."
>
> Newt Gingrich has taken to calling Obama "the best food-stamp president in American history."
>
> Obama, in contrast, says the government must play an increasing role—what he likes to call "shared responsibility"—to ensure a society that is fairer.
>
> Food stamps. This year, more than 46 million (15% of all Americans) will get food stamps. That's 45% higher than when Obama took office, and twice as high as the average for the previous 40 years. This surge was driven in part by the recession, but also because Obama boosted the benefit amount as part of his stimulus plan.[131]

Do you understand now why record gun sales are at record levels across the country? Do you understand now why people are

---

[130] Associated Press, "Food-stamp fraud."
[131] Merline, "Is President Obama Creating."

losing faith in the government, with an increasing number of individuals believing that society is spiraling toward collapse?

The Day the EBT Card Runs Out is the impetus behind such entertainment as *The Walking Dead*. In the past two years Atlanta and Detroit both provided glimpses of the people who rely on entitlements (Dallas as well): it was a monochromatic scene of sadness.

Tick . . . tick . . . tick. . . .

That sound you hear is the timer clocking inexorably to the moment when the bomb goes off—the moment the EBT card stops working at McDonald's; when the EBT card no longer purchase an Enchirito at Taco Bell; when the EBT card no longer supplies steak and lobster; when the song "it's free, swipe your EBT" becomes a reminder of better days; when the EBT card can no longer be used to barter for drugs in Detroit.

This nightmarish scenario will unfold. Barker, King, Romero—any of the various incarnations of *Paranormal Activity* or *Saw* will be child's play when compared to the horror that happens on *Night of the Dead EBT*.

37

"The Capitalist Will Sell You the Rope to Hang Him With": JP Morgan Chase, McDonald's, Walmart, and the EBT/SNAP/Food Stamp Marriage

We already know JP Morgan Chase administers the whole EBT/SNAP/Food Stamp scam, to the tune of between a $0.31 to $2.30 fee per recipient (per individual processing fee, which adds up quickly and can be a fine, profitable business for both executives hoping for higher quarterly profits and investors looking for greater profit margins).

We already know two of the largest private employers in America, Walmart and McDonald's, actively promote welfare and EBT/SNAP/Food Stamps for their employees. It's even part of Walmart's growth strategy and inventory forecasts (revenue management) to factor in EBT/Welfare-dependent customers (it could be argued Walmart is indebted to a continued growth of those reliant on entitlement programs to expand):

Bill Simon, CEO of Wal-Mart's U.S. business, at a Goldman Sachs conference last week, on behavior at a Walmart store around midnight at the end of a month:

"The paycheck cycle we've talked about before remains extreme. It is our responsibility to figure out how to sell in that environment, adjusting pack sizes, large pack at sizes the beginning of the month, small pack sizes at the end of the month. And to figure out how to deal with what is an ever-increasing amount of transactions being paid for with government assistance.

"And you need not go further than one of our stores on midnight at the end of the month. And it's real interesting to watch, about 11 p.m., customers start to come in and shop, fill their grocery basket with basic items, baby formula, milk, bread, eggs, and continue to shop and mill about the store until midnight, when electronic government electronic benefits cards get activated and then the checkout starts and occurs. And our sales for those first few hours on the first of the month are substantially and significantly higher.

"And if you really think about it, the only reason somebody gets out in the middle of the night and buys baby formula is that they need it, and they've been waiting for it. Otherwise, we are open 24 hours — come at 5 a.m., come at 7 a.m., come at 10 a.m. But if you are there at midnight, you are there for a reason."[132]

Welcome to the new norm.

As the population continues to become darker, we know that more and more unemployable individuals of the non-White hue will increasingly find private employment a pipe dream, thereby relying on a transfer of wealth from the productive (White) population to survive.

The new norm.

Do you understand why big business wants amnesty—more consumers dependent on EBT/SNAP/welfare?

Do you understand why both the GOP and DNC are allied against the historic American majority population—because only Whites have a vested interest in ending Black-Run America?

Do you understand what *The Day the EBT Card Runs Out* truly means yet?

Racial Socialism is upon us, with those vaunted corporations Conservatism Inc. loves to defend (Walmart and

---

[132] Topeditor, "Watching Wal-Mart at Midnight."

McDonald's are so entrepreneurial!) part of an incestuous game of "let's have whitey pay for a Newark World Order nationwide!"

Remember: both McDonald's and Walmart openly brag—in corporate messaging—about their non-White workforce; the former's employees can even call the "McResource line" to learn how to take advantage of whitey's tax-dollars:

McDonald's workers should have no problem qualifying for government programs like food stamps and heating assistance.

The hamburger chain pretty much admits that in a call made by a worker to "McResource"—a helpline set up for its workers.

The advocacy group Low Pay is not Ok recorded a phone call made to the helpline by one McDonald's worker Nancy Salgado. The group circulated an edited video of the recording. McDonald's said the video was "not an accurate portrayal of the resource line" because it was "very obviously" edited.

However, CNNMoney reviewed the full recording of the call.

Salgado, who has worked at a Chicago McDonald's for 10 years and makes $8.25 an hour, asked the McResource representative a number of questions related to getting assistance to pay for her heating bill, her groceries and her sister's medical expenses.

Salgado told the representative that she was recording the call for her sister.

The helpline operator never asked Salgado how much she made per hour, and how many hours per week she worked beyond the fact that she was a full-time employee. But she said that Salgado "definitely should be able to qualify for both food stamps and heating assistance."

The representative then pointed her toward a number of resources in Chicago, such as food pantries and a program that would help cover some of her heating bill. She said she would email her specific phone numbers and programs.

The operator also explained that the McResource line is available to help McDonald's workers who need help navigating the process of getting public assistance. The help-line's phone number is posted in fliers at many McDonald's locations.

McDonald's said in a statement that "the McResource Line is intended to be a free, confidential service to help employees and their families get answers to a variety of questions or provide resources on a variety of topics including housing, child care, transportation, grief, elder care, education and more."[133]

In summary: two of America's top ten private employers openly advocate for their employees to get on EBT/SNAP/Welfare, with one of those companies bragging in conference calls about the rate of commerce at the first of the month (because of entitlement abuse); another private company has the contract for EBT/SNAP, which awards them between $0.31 and $2.30 each time they process an individual card. Do you understand why no one truly opposes the growth in Food Stamp usage?[134]

Racial Socialism 101. You're paying for your own dispossession.

Food stamp fraud? Who cares? JPMorgan Chase & Co still gets a processing fee in the end!

Right?

Left?

Republican?

Democrat?

All one can think of is this exchange of dialogue from *Dark Knight Rises*, when the "villain" takes over the Gotham City's Stock Exchange:

[Bane's men announce their entry into the stock exchange, as the food delivery man shoots down a trader, while the

133 Fox, "McDonald's helps workers."
134 Durden, "The Subsidy Addiction."

shoeshiner and janitor fire their guns into the trading screen. As the screens shut off, Bane comes in and walks over to one trader]

Trader #1: This is a stock exchange! There's no money you can steal!

Bane: Really? Then why are you people here?

38

Will White America Ever Shrug? 50.9 Percent of Black
Households and 53.3 Percent of Hispanic Households Live Off
Government Assistance

October 30th, 2013

Are you sitting down?
Go ahead, sit down.
Take your time.
Seated yet?
Good.

We already know *The Day the EBT Card Runs Out* is the
day nature pimp-slaps nurture and the entitlement culture of
Black-Run America, sending our egalitarian society crashing
to the floor; no interference by the state can deny this eventuality from happening.

American Thinker published a powerful essay, "No Demagoguery Needed," which helps explain in lurid detail the enormous costs of shouldering a demographic group ill-equipped to
compete in the cognitively demanding country created (and
sustained) by Whites. Sure, individual Black people can compete, but you don't base social policy on individuals. Here's
what was published at *American Thinker*:

At the end of last week, conservative news media reported
on Census Bureau data showing that there were more people on welfare in the United States than there were people
with full time jobs at the end of 2011. This is alarming news,

but there is also a temptation to make it even more alarming by twisting the numbers to exaggerate the extent that Americans (which in the Census includes non-citizens who simply live in the U.S.) are dependent on government largesse. Terence P. Jeffrey, writing for CNS News, let the facts speak for themselves. He properly cited the Census definition of "means tested benefits" which equate with the popular understanding of welfare programs that transfer goods, services and income to the poor.

According to the Census data cited by Jeffrey, "in the fourth quarter of 2011 were 82,457,000 people in households receiving Medicaid, 49,073,000 beneficiaries of food stamps, 20,223,000 on Supplemental Security Income, 23,228,000 in the Women, Infants and Children program, 13,433,000 in public or subsidized rental housing, and 5,854,000 in the Temporary Assistance for Needy Families program. Also among the 108,592,000 means-tested benefit recipients counted by the Census Bureau were people getting free or reduced-price lunch or breakfast, state-administered supplemental security income and means-tested veterans pensions."

In comparison, 101,716,000 people worked full-time in 2011.

There are other useful figures from the same Census report that did not make the CNS or Newsmax stories. The government figures were broken down by race. While 20.5% of White and 27.9% of Asian households receive some form of means-tested benefits, 50.9% of Black households and 53.3% of Hispanic households receive welfare assistance. The figure for Hispanic households should dispel any notions that the Republican Party will gain any advantage from immigration reforms that increase the size of this voting bloc. Communities with a high dependence on welfare will vote for the party that promises to keep the benefits flowing. There is a reason every Democrat in Congress supports comprehensive immigration reform that would open a path to the voting booth to those who came into the country illegally.[135]

Kudos to William R. Hawkins for bringing to light this information, but even he left out some incredible details. Let's roll the ugliness, data that demonstrates beyond a shadow of a doubt that our tax-dollars could be fueling space exploration— we could have been on Mars—but instead go to fueling 2013 Detroit.

From the 2010 US Census, we learn from "Table 543. Persons Living in Households Receiving Selected Noncash Benefit" that:

- 20.5 percent of whites, 27.9 percent of Asians, 50.9 percent of blacks, and 53.3 percent of Hispanics (Latinos) received means-tested assistance (this includes means-tested cash assistance, food stamps, Medicaid, and public or authorized housing).
- From that same dataset, we learn that 6.9 percent of whites, 18.8 percent of Hispanics (Latinos), 5.7 percent of Asians, and 25.1 percent of blacks live in a household that receives food stamps/EBT/SNAP.
- Crunching the numbers just a tad farther, we learn that 16.7 percent of whites, 43.8 percent of Hispanics (Latinos), 23.2 percent of Asians, and 39.4 percent of blacks live in a household in which on or more persons are covered by Medicaid.
- How about public housing? 1.9 percent of whites, 4.7 percent of Hispanics (Latinos), 2.5 percent of Asians, and 11.5 percent of blacks live in public or authorized housing.
- And, 4.4 percent of whites, 8.7 percent of Hispanics (Latinos), 5.6 percent of Asians, and 13.6 percent of blacks live in a household that receives means-tested cash assistance.

---

[135] Hawkins, "No Demagoguery Needed."

Welcome to America, a land brimming with exceptionalism. Right?

Where we disembarked from a trajectory of working to improve the lives of the historic American majority population, to importing a new underclass less violent than the one we foolishly brought to this continent centuries ago (well, it should be noted their kinsman in Africa willingly parted with some of them, by selling them into slavery).

Now, 50.9 percent of black households (this doesn't take into the account the vast Black prison population, incarcerated to protect what little liberty still exists in America) rely on assistance, with the budding minority group (soon to be a majority in states like California, Texas, Arizona, etc.) known as "Hispanics" seeing 53.3 percent of their households receiving benefits.

Meanwhile, White households are busy supporting this whole scheme.

If 25.1 percent of Black households relied on the EBT/SNAP card for food in 2010, what do you think the percentage is today? Easily, the number is north of 35 percent.

Easily.

Are you still sitting down?

Why?

You have work to do, for the Black underclass (and brown) needs your assistance via a racial tax/transfer of wealth.

American exceptionalism in 2013 means everyone in America has a future, except White Americans.

Bibliography

AAP (Australian Associated Press). "Detroit witness: 'Kill the dude.'" *The Age*, May 28, 2011. https://tinyurl.com/mpkk6x85.

Adversity. "2007 Edition: U.S. Office of Personnel Management Report." Adversity.net, July 23, 2007. https://tinyurl.com/2ahh2kwt.

Associated Press. "Food-stamp fraud: Detroit-area stores swipe millions from aid program." *MLive*, March 1, 2010. https://tinyurl.com/425p96ny.

Associated Press. "Is Martin Luther King Jr.'s dream a reality? In changed Birmingham, yes and no." *Associated Press*, August 24, 2013. https://tinyurl.com/42hpf68y.

Associated Press. "Marching for King's dream: 'The task is not done.'" *Associated Press*, August 24, 2013. https://tinyurl.com/2a52wz36.

Associated Press. "Poor Give Reminder of Earth's Ills." *The Post Standard*, July 17, 1969.

Atkinson, Joseph D. *The Real Stuff: History of National Aeronautics and Space Administration's Astronaut Recruitment Programme: A History of NASA's Astronaut Recruitment Program*. Praeger, 1985.

Auster, Lawrence. "What Blacks Contribute to Civilization." *View from the Right*, April 15, 2012. http://www.amnation.com/vfr/archives/022187.html.

Ballasy, Nicholas. "Sessions: Food stamp spending up 100 percent since Obama took office." *Daily Caller*, June 7, 2012. https://tinyurl.com/2eswew6h.

Beene, Ryan. "Detroit's public schools post worst scores on record in national assessment." *Crains Detroit Business*, December 8, 2009. https://tinyurl.com/r37b3yj8.

Bennett, Lerone Jr. "The Sculptor Who Would Have Gone into Space." *Ebony*, February 1984.

Black Voice News. "HBCU Morgan State University Shares in $95.8 Million Grant from NASA." *Black Voice News*, April 11, 2011. https://tinyurl.com/wh4z59jc.

Bloch, Michael, et al. "Food Stamp Usage Across the Country." *The New York Times*, November 28, 2009. https://tinyurl.com/2mxyyc3a.

Bolden, Charles F. "NASA Policy Statement on Diversity and Inclusion." National Aeronautics and Space Administration, June 8, 2010. https://tinyurl.com/3w8mdvzs.

Booker, Simeon. Editorial comment. *Jet*, July 31, 1969.

Brown, Alex, and National Journal. "Here's How NASA Thinks Society Will Collapse." *The Atlantic,* March 18, 2014. https://tinyurl.com/3xtjxsxs.

Burgess, Lisa. "Despite recruitment efforts, few black pilots land in Air Force, Navy cockpits." *Stars and Stripes,* June 22, 2003. https://tinyurl.com/7fx8259w.

Butler, Orville and Kenneth Lipartito. *A History of the Kennedy Space Center.* University Press of Florida, 2007.

CBS/AP. "Computer Glitch Blamed For Nationwide EBT System Shutdown On Saturday." *CBS Boston,* October 12, 2013. https://tinyurl.com/52n4ff5z.

Chafets, Ze'ev. *Devil's Night: And Other True Tales of Detroit.* New York: Random House, 1990.

Chaikin, Andrew. *A Man on the Moon: The Voyages of the Apollo Astronauts.* New York: Viking, 1994.

Childs, Arcynta Ali. "How Nichelle Nichols Launched Real-Time Opportunities for Women in Space." *Smithsonian Magazine,* June 23, 2011. https://tinyurl.com/yceytyws.

Christian Science Monitor. "Both Moon and Earth." *The Christian Science Monitor,* August 5, 1969.

Collins, Michael. *Carrying the Fire: An Astronaut's Journeys.* New York: Farrar, Straus and Giroux, 1974.

Dade, Corey. "Government Job Cuts Threaten Black Middle Class." NPR, May 9, 2012. https://tinyurl.com/r2u4hzx5.

Daily Kos. "On Diversity, NASA Lags Behind. New Poll." *Daily Kos,* May 31, 2009.

Deadline Detroit. "At Utash Court Hearing, Suspects' Relatives Laugh At Assault Details." *Deadline Detroit,* April 21, 2014. https://tinyurl.com/2cs7a49h.

DeGroot, Gerard. *Dark Side of the Moon: The Magnificent Madness of the American Lunar Quest.* New York: New York University Press, 2006.

DeGroot, Gerard (Jerry). "The Space Race Is a Pointless Waste of Money." *The Telegraph,* February 25, 2009. https://tinyurl.com/ms865z2h.

DeParle, Jason and Robert Gebeloff. "Food Stamp Use Soars, and Stigma Fades." *The New York Times,* November 28, 2009. https://www.nytimes.com/2009/11/29/us/29foodstamps.html

Derbyshire, John. "On Maya Angelou, Ta-Nehisi Coates: The Whining Of Pampered Pets." *VDARE,* May 29, 2014. https://tinyurl.com/yrwmehkf.

Dick, Steven K., and Roger D. Launius, eds. *The Societal Impact of Spaceflight.* Washington, D.C.: NASA History Division, 2007.

Dolan, Matthew. "Detroit's Water Cutoffs Spark Protests." *The Wall Street Journal,* July 18, 2014. https://tinyurl.com/yjbhcnv2.

Dunar, Andrew J. and Stephen P. Waring. *Power to Explore: a History of Marshall Space Flight Center, 1960-1990.* Washington, DC: National Aeronautics and Space Administration, NASA History Office, Office of Policy and Plans, 1999.

Durden, Tyler. "The Subsidy Addiction: Jobs Vs Foodstamps." *Zero Hedge,* February 5, 2013. https://tinyurl.com/2xhx6n49.

Dwight, Edward. *Soaring on the Wings of a Dream: the Untold Story of America's First Black Astronaut.* Denver: Self-Published, 2009.

Ebony Magazine. "How Blacks View Mankind's 'Giant Step': Space scientists, laymen see space program from different perspective." *Ebony,* September 1970.

Edgerton, Gary. *The Columbia History of American Television.* New York: Columbia University Press, 2007.

Fekadu, Mesfin. "Randy Newman writes new satirical, political song." *The Daytona Beach News-Journal,* September 18, 2012. https://tinyurl.com/yf5ps3hx.

Fincannon, James. "Six Flags on the Moon: What is Their Current Condition?" *Apollo Lunar Surface Journal,* April 2012. http://www.hq.nasa.gov/alsj/ApolloFlags-Condition.html

Foust, Jeff. "NASA Facing New Space Science Cuts," *National Geographic,* May 31, 2014. https://tinyurl.com/4dwyj3ws.

Fox News. "NASA Chief: Next Frontier Is Better Relations With Muslim World." *Fox News,* July 5, 2010. https://tinyurl.com/c4p33bhv.

Fox, Emily Jane. "McDonald's helps workers get food stamps." *CNN Business,* October 24, 2013. https://tinyurl.com/3v876ynj.

Grey, Justin. "Clayton Food Stamp Snafu Angers Many." *My Fox Atlanta,* August 11, 2011. https://tinyurl.com/4upatyr9.

Haley, Alex. "Alex Haley Interviews Martin Luther King, Jr." *Playboy,* January 1965.

Halper, Daniel. "Report: US Spent $3.7 Trillion on Welfare Over Last 5 Years." *The Weekly Standard,* October 23, 2013. https://tinyurl.com/3macdsva.

Harrington, Elizabeth. "USDA Creating $1.9 Million Research Center Devoted to Changing American's Food Choices." *Free Beacon,* April 9, 2018. https://tinyurl.com/mv8rtdpf.

Harris, Ruth Bates. *Harlem Princess: The Story of Harry Delaney's Daughter.* New York: T. Nelson, 1993.

Hawkins, William R. "No Demagoguery Needed." *American Thinker,* October 30, 2013. https://tinyurl.com/mssdkp3z.

Heppenheimer, T. A. *The Space Shuttle Decision: NASA's Search for a Reusable Space Vehicle.* Cia Publishing, 1999.

Hersch, Matthew H. *Inventing the American Astronaut.* Palgrave McMillan, 2012.

Holden, Constance. "NASA: Sacking of Top Black Woman Stirs Concern for Equal Employment." *Science* 182, no. 4114 (November 1973). https://doi.org/10.1126/science.182.4114.804.a.

Hopkins, Billy. *Apollo Moon Missions: The Unsung Heroes.* Bison Books, 2007.

Hunter, Marcus. "House Fire Leaves 1 Dead, 1 in Hospital." *My Fox Memphis*, November 10, 2009. https://tinyurl.com/yzdy3vvv.

Indianapolis Recorder, The. November 11, 1973.

Instauration. "Faustian Lapse." *Instauration,* June 1980.

Instauration. "NASA: The Rocket versus the Mule." *Instauration,* July 1978.

Instauration. "The Road To Infinity: The Race Factor in Space Flight." *Instauration,* July 1980.

Izzo, Phil. "Food-Stamp Use Rises; Some 15% Get Benefits." *The Wall Street Journal,* August 9, 2013. https://www.wsj.com/articles/BL-REB-19884.

Jagernauth, Kevin. "Watch: First Trailer For Christopher Nolan's 'Interstellar' Starring Matthew McConaughey, Jessica Chastain & Many More." *IndieWire*, December 14, 2013. https://tinyurl.com/24nu9xx7.

Jenkins, Harriet G. Interview by Jennifer Ross-Nazzal. *NASA Headquarters Oral History Project,* August 5, 2011. https://tinyurl.com/55cvd5xy.

Jet Magazine, November 15, 1973.

Jet Magazine, September 20, 1974.

Jet Magazine. "Blacks Scarce as Men on Moon at Launch." *Jet Magazine,* July 31, 1969.

Jet Magazine. "League's New Goal to be 'Ghetto Power in Action.'" *Jet Magazine,* August 4, 1969.

Jet Magazine. "Giant Leap for Mankind." Photo editorial, *Jet Magazine,* September 1969.

Johnson, Thomas A. "Blacks and Apollo: Most Couldn't Have Cared Less." *The New York Times*, July 27, 1969, https://tinyurl.com/mdwv95aa.

Jones, Joyce. "Government Shutdown Hits Blacks Where They Already Hurt." *Bet.com*, October 2, 2013. https://tinyurl.com/528ebcdy.

Journal of Blacks in Higher Education, The. "Tracking Graduation Rates at HBCUs." *The Journal of Blacks in Higher Education*, January 5, 2012. https://www.jbhe.com/2012/01/tracking-graduation-rates-at-hbcus/.

Judicial Watch. "U.S. Pours Millions into Failing Black Colleges, Breaks New Student Loan Rules." Judicial Watch, March 19, 2013. https://tinyurl.com/2wx3an66.

Kaysing, Bill. "The Wrong Stuff." *Wired*, September 1994. https://www.billkaysing.com/thewrongstuff.php.

Kersey, Paul. "Prospects for Racial Separation." *The Occidental Quarterly*, Fall 2010. https://toqonline.com/archives/v10n3/TOQv10n3Kersey.pdf.

Kersey, Paul. "Segregation: What "Red Tails' and the Tuskegee Airmen Story Really Celebrated." *The Unz Review*, January 12, 2012. https://www.unz.com/sbpdl/what-red-tailsand-tuskegee-airmen-story/.

Kersey, Paul. "Wilkes-Barre, Pennsylvania: the Black Undertow Cometh." *The Unz Review,* October 22, 2013. https://tinyurl.com/3m7w3t5h.

Knowles, David. "Forsaken Detroit homes for sale for as little as $1." *New York Daily News*, August 1, 2013. https://tinyurl.com/58wv846u.

Launius, Roger D. "Denying the Apollo Moon Landings: Conspiracy and Questioning in Modern American History." *Smithsonian Institute*, October 2009. https://tinyurl.com/2cahefmp.

Madrigal, Alexis C. "Moondoggle: The Forgotten Opposition to the Apollo Program." *The Atlantic*, September 13, 2012. https://tinyurl.com/2rjnc896.

Mailer, Norman. *Of a Fire on the Moon*. Boston: Little, Brown, 1970.

Martinez-Schiferl, Michael. "WIC Participants and Their Growing Need for Coverage." Urban Institute, April 2012. https://tinyurl.com/47thvy2z.

McCurdy, Howard E. *High Technology and Organizational Change in the U.S. Space Program*. John Hopkins University Press, 1996.

McGaughty, Lauren. "Next step on food stamp fraud up to Wal-Mart, local police say." *Nola.com*, October 15, 2013. https://tinyurl.com/wyx9msxd.

Merline, John. "Is President Obama Creating A Nation Of Dependents?" *Investor's Business Daily*, January 29, 2012. https://tinyurl.com/2x6zuhb6.

MIAC. "Main Pages." MIAC Network, Accessed January 6, 2009. https://tinyurl.com/2p9rmwmm.

Moskowitz, Clara. "NASA chief says agency's goal is Muslim outreach, forgets to mention space." *The Christian Science Monitor*, July 14, 2010. https://tinyurl.com/2w7xdnka.

Museveni, Yoweri. "Africans must travel to the moon: Uganda president." AFP, May 2, 2009. https://tinyurl.com/34jpy8t6.

National Aeronautics and Space Administration. "NASA Awards $17.6 Million for Minority University Science and Technology Programs." Press release, December 14, 2010. https://tinyurl.com/ynxhyje9.

National Aeronautics and Space Administration. "NASA Celebrates the 50th Anniversary of the Civil Rights Act of 1964." NASA, July 2, 2014. https://tinyurl.com/2a2uz594.

National Aeronautics and Space Administration. "NASA Selects Minority University Teams for 2014 Microgravity Research Flights." Press release, June 16, 2014. https://tinyurl.com/mptxxbw4.

National Aeronautics and Space Administration. *Wings in Orbit: Scientific and Engineering Legacies of the Space Shuttle, 1971–2010*. Johnson Space Center, Houston, Texas.

NCPA. "The Consequences of the 'Great Society.'" National Center for Policy Analysis, July 10, 2014. https://tinyurl.com/2p84zjwp.

Neufeld, Michael. *Von Braun: Dreamer of Space, Engineer of War*. Vintage Reprint, 2008.

Nye, David E. *Narratives and Spaces: Technology and the Construction of American Culture*. New York: Columbia University Press, 1997.

Office of Public Affairs. "Attorney General Eric Holder Delivers Remarks at the National Action to Realize the Dream March." The United States Department of Justice, August 24, 2013. https://tinyurl.com/wzrf9m97.

Paletta, Damian, and Caroline Porter. "Use of Food Stamps Swells Even as Economy Improves." *The Wall Street Journal*, March 27, 2013. https://tinyurl.com/2wwfzc69.

Paul, Richard. "How NASA Joined the Civil Rights Revolution: Integration came to the nation's space agency in the mid-1960s." *Smithsonian Magazine*, March 2014. https://tinyurl.com/4exubyw7.

Perry, Imani. "For the Poor People's Campaign, the Moonshot Was Less Than a Triumph." *The New York Times*, July 16, 2019. https://tinyurl.com/5yuwku2v.

Perry, Ruth. "Opinion: Health of Trenton residents is closely linked to access to quality education." *True Jersey*, November 13, 2013. https://tinyurl.com/yt65ud66.

Phelps, Alfred J. *They Had a Dream: The Story of African-American Astronauts*. Novato, CA: Presidio, 1994.

Pizzi, Jenna. "Aramark to offer Trenton students in after-school programs free dinner beginning this fall." *NJ.com,* June 12, 2014. https://tinyurl.com/4ycnzfpw.

Plummer, William, David Grogan, and Denise Lynch. "Where We Were." *People*, November 28, 1988. https://tinyurl.com/yzrw4wav.

Roy, Caroline. "Walmart shelves in Springhill, Mansfield, cleared in EBT glitch." *KSLA News 12*, October 14, 2013. https://tinyurl.com/3e6cxa6u.

Rutledge, Doris. Letter to the editor. *Ebony,* October 1969.

Ryan, Andrea. "EBT System Goes Down: Obama Voters Threaten Mass Riots." *The Gateway Pundit,* October 12, 2013, https://tinyurl.com/banue8sn.

Safire, William to H. R. Haldeman. "In Event of Moon Disaster." July 18, 1969. Memorandum. From National Archives. https://tinyurl.com/2427n9ka.

Sailer, Steve. "The Atlanta School Scandal: After a Year, Chamber of Commerce (aka Conservatism, Inc.) Doesn't Want to Talk About It." *VDARE*, July 7, 2011. https://tinyurl.com/388w7f3p.

Schuppe, Jonathon. "Newarkers take Altoona express, Pa. city is none too pleased." *Star Ledger,* June 1, 2007.

Schweizer, Peter. "JP Morgan's Food Stamp Empire." *Daily Beast*, October 1, 2012. https://www.thedailybeast.com/jp-morgans-food-stamp-empire.

Shepardson, David. "Detroit, feds talk up to $100M for blight funding." *The Detroit News*, April 16, 2014. https://tinyurl.com/3pv2f4v8.

Shyler, David J. *Women in Space—Following Valentina*. Springer: 2005.

Slayton, Donald K. and Michael Cassutt. *Deke!: U.S. Manned Space: From Mercury to the Shuttle*. New York: Forge, 1994.

Smith, Nona E. Letter to the editor. *Ebony,* October 1969.

Smith, Rich. "Russia Bans U.S. From International Space Station: How Should America Respond?" *The Motley Fool*, June 7, 2014. https://tinyurl.com/4n73nuhc.

Stephens, Challen. "FBI Asking Questions About What Happened in Greene County." *AL.com*, October 29, 2010. https://tinyurl.com/mprpmeuu.

Sullivan, Walter. "Trend Studied as Fewer Blacks Choose Sciences." *The New York Times*, September 23, 1986. https://tinyurl.com/muwhv9yn.

Tennis, Joe. "Banking on Memories in Coalwood, W.Va." *Herald Courier*, August 17, 2008. https://tinyurl.com/ef5ndtfs.

Thompson, Mark A. "Space Race: African American Newspapers Respond to Sputnik and Apollo 11." Master's thesis, University of North Texas, 2007.

Topeditor. "Watching Wal-Mart at Midnight." *The Wall Street Journal*, September 20, 2010. https://tinyurl.com/2ke4bcvd.

US Census Bureau. Persons Living in Households Receiving Selected noncash Benefits, Table 543. US Census 2010. https://tinyurl.com/je3rckpd.

US Department of the Treasury. "Treasury Announces $3.5 Billion in New Markets Tax Credit Awards to Revitalize Low-Income and Distressed Communities." Press release, April 24, 2013. https://home.treasury.gov/news/press-releases/jl1912.

Wallace, Hunter. "Black Apocalypse." *Occidental Dissent*, May 10, 2011. https://tinyurl.com/e9rhhnn4.

Washington Post. "Racism, Sexism, and Space Ventures." *Washington Post*, 24 November, 1973.

Washington Post. "Senators Eye NASA EEO Goals." *Washington Post*, January 25, 1974.

Williams, Timonthy. "As Public Sector Sheds Jobs, Blacks Are Hit Hardest." *The New York Times*, November 28, 2011. https://tinyurl.com/y8bebwz7.

Winerip, Michael. "For Detroit Schools, Mixed Picture on Reforms." *The New York Times*, March 13, 2011. https://tinyurl.com/yn8rx9u6.

Wolfe, Tom. *The Right Stuff*. New York: Farrar, Straus, and Giroux, 1979.

Wright, Harley. "Obama White House Awards HBCUs, but How Will the Money be Managed." *Michigan Chronicle*, September 25, 2012.

Yeager, Chuck and Leo Janos. *Yeager: An Autobiography*. Toronto: Bantam Books, 1985.

ENJOYED THIS BOOK?

TO READ MORE, VISIT US AT

ANTELOPEHILLPUBLISHING.COM